DISCIPLINE
in Christian Classrooms

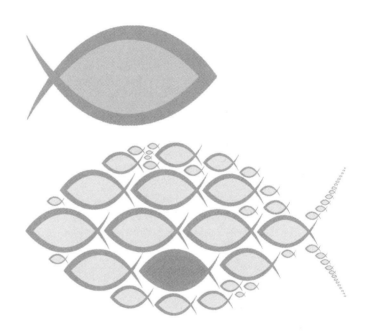

Practical Suggestions from the Field

CONCORDIA PUBLISHING HOUSE · SAINT LOUIS

Text of readings by Jeffrey E. Burkart, Dee Christopher, David
Ebeling, Michael Eschelbach, Rebecca Fisher, Jane Fryar,
Gretchen Gebhardt, Drew Gerdes, James Gimbel, Lyla Glaskey,
Matthew C. Harrison, Marlene Krohse, Paul McCain, Tom Num-
mela, Rodney Rathmann, Julie Stiegemeyer, Martha Streufert
Jander, Mindy Walz, Judy Williams, and Karen Wittmayer.

Questions by Mark S. Sengele

Editors: Thomas A. Nummela and Mark S. Sengele

Adapted from articles in *Teachers Interaction* magazine,
2000–2013, copyright © Concordia Publishing House. All rights
reserved.

1 2 3 4 5 6 7 8 9 10   23 22 21 20 19 18 17 16 15 14

Table of Contents

Introduction: What Is Discipline?

Webster's dictionary defines *discipline* as (1) training that corrects, molds, or perfects the mental faculties or moral character; (2) self-control. Thus *disciplining* means to train or develop by instruction and exercise, especially in self-control. In the language of Scripture, a disciple is a follower of Jesus.

Hebrews 12 teaches, "The Lord disciplines the one He loves, and chastises every son whom He receives" (v. 6). God lovingly cherishes and disciplines us so that our relationship with Him may be maintained and His purpose accomplished. "[God] disciplines us for our good, that we may share His holiness. For the moment all discipline seems painful rather than pleasant, but later it yields the peaceful fruit of righteousness" (vv. 10–11).

The Holy Spirit strengthens our faith through Word and Sacraments, preparing us for eternal salvation and enabling us to be thankful for the sufferings and hardships in life, rather than resentful of them. Our heavenly Father strengthens and encourages us through times of suffering and trial evidencing His love and care.

For the Sunday School teacher, disciplining and discipling go hand in hand. As you prepare to teach your lessons, keep in mind that in order to disciple, you may have to discipline.

The goal of Christ-centered discipline is always the student's well-being. The Law must be applied so that, after repentance, the growing disciple may realize again the comfort and assurance of forgiveness found in the Gospel.

Through your words and actions, remind children of their baptismal grace, forgiveness, and renewal of a right relationship with Jesus. During those times when you feel like you are disciplining more than you are teaching, remind yourself that disciplining and discipling go hand in hand. As God's redeemed children, we are disciplined so that we might repent of our sins and grow in our Christian life.

May the Holy Spirit inspire you and fill you with His grace and knowledge as you sharpen and improve your teaching skills!

How could I use this resource?

- Use the articles individually or in a group.
- Study one article at a time, or do a few related ones together.
- Discuss or ponder the beginning thought.
- Consider how the article impacts teaching the Christian faith.
- Talk about how the content applies to your setting.

Section1

Planning for Discipline Success

Blessed is the man whom You discipline,
O Lord, and whom You teach out of Your law.

Psalm 94:12

Plan to Succeed

Mindy Walz

OPENING THOUGHT

How does the age of your students impact your lesson planning?

Review

"It's another discipline article (sigh). I get so tired of consequences. I just want to teach." Did you find yourself thinking similar thoughts when you turned the page? I hope not, but many volunteers who work with kids struggle with maintaining order.

Doling out consequences and punishments is often the first thing that comes to mind when considering discipline. That really should be a last resort. One of the first things to consider as a discipline tool is thorough planning. Teaching without planning may prove to be a recipe for trouble. While you decide what to do, your students have unstructured downtime. Most groups have at least some kids who quickly find things to do during that time. Unfortunately, their choices are often distracting and sometimes even destructive. Regaining order can become an uphill battle for the rest of the class time. Kids who are actively engaged in meaningful activities usually cause far less trouble.

Transitions

When planning for a class or event, think through transition times carefully. Which activities connect naturally to each other? If you have a whole-group opening time, can you have an activity all laid out and ready to go for when your group gets to that spot? Can you prepare a small bag with all of the materials for a craft or activity for each child instead of passing out one thing at a time? The less time that passes between activities, the better.

Consider the average attention span of the group you are working with. Generally speaking, the younger the child, the shorter the attention span. Plan different types of activities, and try to be prepared with more material than you think you will need. That way, you can watch the kids for cues. Move on if you have been doing one thing for a while and you can tell students are starting to lose interest. Stick with what you are doing if they are really into it. Do your best to make sure kids are involved in meaningful activities from the time they arrive until they leave.

Attention Span

Older students do have a longer attention span, but using various activities is still a good idea. Changing things up keeps it interesting. Try to consider what would make the lesson fun for you if you were in your students' shoes. If you think the activity is interesting, the kids are more likely to remain interested also.

Yes, it is a lot of work to put this kind of effort into planning and preparing a lesson or activity, but it is worth it in the long run. Many discipline issues can be avoided entirely by putting in the up-front work of thorough planning. Being confident because you have thoroughly planned and prepared will help you love the work you have been called to do—and the kids you have been called to work with—even more!

Think About

- When it comes to planning, I . . .

- How could you change your planning strategy depending on the age of your students?

- How will you improve your planning?

- What does planning look like to you? to others?

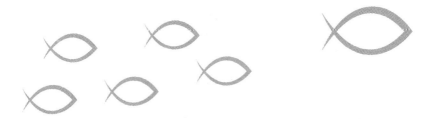

The Six *P*s of Discipline

Karen Wittmayer

Review

The Bible teaches us that God disciplines us for our own good because He loves us. Therefore, out of love and concern for the children in our Sunday School classes, we seek a discipline program that will promote a caring, instructive environment. This process becomes more complicated when a child with special needs is in the class.

Most children, including those with special needs, will respond well to consistently applied rules about showing respect to teachers, classmates, and property. Keep this in mind when developing a discipline plan for your Sunday School.

- **Pray:** Pray for the wisdom that only God can impart and for insights into all your students, especially those with special needs.

- **Plan:** Determine how you want your class to operate. What should the children do as soon as they enter the class? How should they respond to the teacher's questions during lesson time? How will the children be allowed to treat one another and you?

- **Post:** Develop and post a set of six rules for your class. Phrase each rule in the positive, stating what is allowed or expected, in language at the level of the children. Review these rules every week.

- **Praise:** As you observe the children in your class following the rules, praise them. Praise even small steps toward a desired behavior. Praise students individually or as a group, stating what it is that they are doing well.

- **Prevent:** In football, they say, "A good defense is a strong offense." This is also true in the classroom. Monitor behavior and redirect or separate students before a problem occurs.

- **Personalize:** Personalize your discipline plan for the child with special needs. Seat the child near you during class time. Develop a secret cue to refocus the child. Meet with the child's parents to find out what works at home. Create a "thinking chair" for time-outs. Possibly even have the parent(s) come into the classroom and then observe how they work with their special needs child. Make the special child a helper in order to give breaks during the class time. Ask for help from your superintendent or a trained professional from your congregation when you feel overwhelmed.

Finally, always remember that you are not in the classroom alone. Our Lord is always with you. The Holy Spirit is constantly working through God's Word, in you and in the children of your class, so that all may continue to grow in their knowledge, faith, and love for our awesome God.

Think About

- The most important step is . . .

- Which of the six *P*s would you concentrate on first?

- How could you adapt this plan for your teaching situation?

- How could knowing your students better help you plan better?

The Substitute

David Ebeling

OPENING THOUGHT

What's the biggest challenge for a substitute teacher?

Review

Almost every Sunday School class needs a substitute teacher from time to time. Class management can be a bigger challenge to the substitute than teaching the actual content for the day's lesson. Children generally like routine. They can count on it. The regular teacher has a routine. When it is disrupted by a substitute, the opportunities for misbehavior dramatically increase.

The Teacher

If you are the regular teacher, here are some things you can do to help your substitute have a successful class and be willing to be your sub sometime in the future.

- Keep your teaching materials organized and labeled.

- Prepare a name tent or badge for each class member. Make it routine for each child to pick up his name tent when he arrives and place it on the table where he is sitting. Then, when a sub arrives some Sunday morning, the routine will make it easier for the sub to call children by name.

- Teach your class to treat any substitute with respect. Remind them to help their sub with unfamiliar issues.

The Substitute

If you are a substitute, consider these suggestions for your next adventure.

- Have a file of paper-and-pencil activities or Bible-related games that you can use to break the ice with your class or occupy the last few minutes of the day.

- Don't let yourself be intimidated by the image of a perfect teacher. No one is that person.

The Superintendent

If you are a superintendent, you can help with a couple of easy steps.

- Go into the classroom with the substitute to introduce her or him to the class, and then stay long enough to know he or she is off to a good start.

- Recruit substitutes in teams of two. One team member could be a student's parent—someone who knows the children well.

Prepare in advance. When the occasion arises and a substitute is needed, you'll be ahead of the game!

Think About

- The next time I need a substitute . . .

- Are you more likely to be the substitute or need a substitute?

- How could you best prepare for a substitute?

- How could you best prepare to be a substitute?

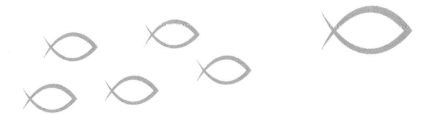

R.E.A.L.I.T.Y. Discipline

David Ebeling

Review

The reality of teaching children is that kids need discipline. Like all of us, they are sinners. They talk out of turn. They hit each other. They don't pay attention. So, we discipline them. We pause as we talk to one child to ask another to wait her turn. We separate two students who can't keep their hands off each other. We talk to their parents when we can't seem to make a significant change in behavior by ourselves.

However, the goal of Christian education is not disciplined children—it is discipling, making disciples, followers of Jesus Christ. We practice discipline to help the learners focus on the reality of God's grace shown in the redemptive work of Jesus. Is discipline a reality in your classroom? Take this R.E.A.L.I.T.Y check.

- **Rules:** When making rules, state the reason for the rule, exactly what the rule means and doesn't mean, and how you'll deal with situations when the rule is violated. Rules are "Law" and Law shows us our sin and need for our Savior.

- **Express:** With your eyes and your voice, express excitement to be with your learners. They'll want to be there if you want to be there. They'll know if you love them because God loved us first.

- **Actions:** Don't wait for trouble. Your actions can keep distractions to a minimum so learning can take place. Anticipate what might go wrong and be prepared with at least one alternative activity.

- **Lead:** Make routine decisions promptly and specifically. If you delay or sound uncertain, the class can become chaotic. Children value a teacher who leads, one who is in charge, one who knows what she or he wants them to learn.

- **Invest:** Know your children well. Engage them in conversation so that you respect their individual needs and differences. They—and their parents—will appreciate your investment in them personally.

- **T**one: Set a pace that is comfortable but dynamic. Change the tone of your teaching every fifteen minutes or less. Think of a one-hour class time as four or five different lessons. Each will be different enough that the children will value the variety.

- **Y**ou: As the teacher, you are the key to the effectiveness of your class. You decide if your emphasis is discipline or discipleship. You use every opportunity to equip them to be followers of Jesus. You share the Good News and model for them what it is to be a disciple.

Think About

- My reality check . . .
- How do discipline and discipling relate?
- Which R.E.A.L.I.T.Y. skill do you do well?
- Which R.E.A.L.I.T.Y. skill do you need to work on?

T Minus Ten and Counting

Rebecca Fisher

OPENING THOUGHT

In the ten minutes before class, I am usually...

Review

In just ten minutes, your students will come bursting into your Sunday School classroom, fully fueled with chocolate doughnuts and the joy of life. You feel the adrenaline surge through your veins—a unique mix of eager anticipation and breath-holding nervousness. But before you get to that point, take your preparedness pulse. How ready are you for your thundering herd? Consider using a preflight checklist. School bus drivers do it. Pilots do it. Teachers, too, can use such a list to make sure things run smoothly.

Ten Things to Check

1. You've read the Scripture passages that frame the story or topic for the day and pondered them in your heart for several days, asking God to lead you to new insights or applications at your students' level.

2. You've gathered all the lesson supplies together in one place already so you can relax and enjoy the children's entrance, speaking to each by name and welcoming any visitors warmly.

3. You've removed any unnecessary furniture or distractions from your classroom or covered them up (bedsheets work well) to help the kids focus.

4. You've practiced using any equipment or teaching tools so you have a high comfort level for smoothness of operation.

5. You've carefully walked through the lesson mentally at least three times during the preceding week so you won't be tied to your book.

6. You know who has a birthday when they walk into the room, and you're prepared with the celebration.

7. You have talked with members of your teaching team before they arrive on Sunday morning so they know their responsibilities and have had adequate time to prepare for them.

8. You have prayed for each of the students during the week, and you have prayed that God would be seen through your instruction and compassion for the students.

9. You have crafted a welcoming atmosphere, whether through the music playing, the activities laid out, the lighting of the room, or its scent. Your students will see right away that they have arrived in a place where they are valued.

10. You have had adequate sleep and are well rested, ready to share God's love at your very best.

Like a pilot, the use of the preflight checklist does not guarantee a successful flight, but it certainly boosts the chances tremendously! You have such a powerful opportunity to share Christ with children who may hear almost nothing about Him other than during this hour each week. Make sure that when they thunder into the classroom, you're absolutely ready to focus on them with the joy of knowing you're as ready as you can be.

Think About

- In the ten minutes before class, I want to . . .

- What easy changes could you make in your classroom?

- How could these steps help you prepare to teach?

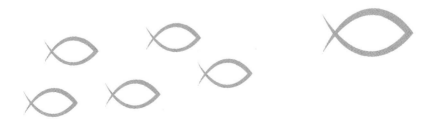

Attention, Please!

Rebecca Fisher

Review

In an early scene of the movie *Dangerous Minds*, we see a stunned first-year teacher reeling from the initial encounter with her challenging students. As she considers giving up, her friend and mentor snaps her back to reality: "Luann, you can teach these kids—but first you have to get their attention."

It's a wise reminder for all teachers! Lack of attention leads to misunderstandings, disciplinary challenges, frustration, and, most tragically, lost opportunity to share the Gospel with students who desperately need to hear the message of unconditional love and acceptance each week.

Let's consider three tools you have to get full attention, all available in your "teacher toolbox" regardless of age group or teaching experience.

Visual Stimuli

Sometimes a well-chosen visual object lesson that connects to the concept you want to teach is exceptionally powerful. My thirty-five seventh graders are packed into a tiny room for Sunday School, so I pull out a lot of object lessons to keep their focus. Last week, we placed a trash bag on the ground where students had been sitting. While talking about the mess that various sins can make in our lives, I squirted ketchup, mustard, maple syrup, and salad dressing on the garbage bag, making a slimy middle-school-friendly goop. You can bet I had their attention! We then thought about how we could clean up the sin mess, and a student dribbled dishwashing detergent on the slime and another tried to scrub it. Of course, that just made it worse, showing that we do not have the power to clean up our own sins. In comes Christ, whose death and resurrection rolled away the trash bag entirely, with no evidence of our sin left.

Life Connections

Using that same visual lesson, and not speaking in generalities about this sin or the other, I spoke of typical sins that middle-school students struggle with: cruelty on the Internet, gossiping about and excluding others at school, shoplifting temptations, and cheating by texting answers to the test. When we make direct connections with the culture in which they swim, it refocuses them, equipping them to connect faith and their lives. It is likely that your curriculum works hard to do this, but you know your students better than publishers do. Adapt freely!

The Power of Story

Invite a member of the congregation to tell his or her faith story for ten minutes. Prepare a series of interview questions to connect that story with the theme of the lesson. Because we love to hear stories, the storyteller gets full attention regardless of age.

Try adding one of these tools to the next lesson you teach. See if it doesn't have the power to get students focused so that the Gospel can be shared in its fullness!

Think About

- You can best get my attention by . . .
- What visual lessons would work best with your students?
- Why is it important to connect the lessons to your students' lives?
- Who could you invite to share their story?

Transitions

Rebecca Fisher

Review

Every lesson you teach will have several points when things are more likely to fall apart and discipline problems may arise. These are the transitions between major components or activities in the lesson. If the transition goes smoothly, no one is likely to notice. If the transition is rough, your carefully planned lesson may fall apart. Teachers are often so busy crafting the major components of the learning time that transitions receive little attention. Yet transitions are the time when most disruptions to the learning process occur, so they deserve our planning just as much as all the other components.

Transitions

Transitioning enables students to flow from one activity to the next without losing focus on the main learning objectives. Start with these questions:

- What physical change of scenery is needed for this next component?

- What change in mood do I wish to implement for this next activity?

- How might I signal our need to shift gears in a respectful and enjoyable way?

- What problems do I foresee in the transition? How can I minimize them?

Plan your transitions accordingly. Keep notes or samples of transition ideas that work well. Strive for some variety, but remember that many students thrive when the class session follows a familiar, predictable path.

Music and Movement

Music, regardless of the class's age, is an effective transitioning tool and mood changer. Train your preschool-aged children to recognize that a particular song, when played on the DVD player, means it's nearly time to move to the next activity and they should start the cleanup process. Invite second graders to prowl like lions to the next activity. If that activity is in the same room, prowl around the tables several times. Kids need to move. If you can connect the animal to the story, that's even better.

Ask middle-grade students to touch three walls and then sit down in a new place for the next portion of the lesson. This stimulates their brain and readies them for what's next!

Make sure all supplies are ready before shifting the students' gears so you engage them immediately in the new activity.

Students of all ages feel more secure if they know what's coming next. A visual road map can help with the transition process. Write a brief agenda on the board, or draw a series of pictures on a poster for that week's lesson.

Carefully planned transitions can often eliminate disruptions entirely. We have our students for such a short time each week. Let's do all we can to minimize lost time and maximize their learning about God's wonderful plan for us.

Think About

- A well-planned transition succeeds because . . .

- How many transitions do you make during your average lesson?

- What types of transitions might work best with your students?

- What kind of musical transitions would most appeal to your students?

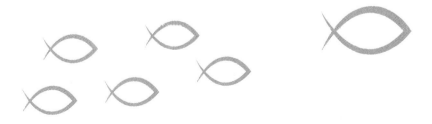

Set Up for Success

Tom Nummela

Review

Discipline is consistently one of the big concerns for volunteer teachers. It is the most frequently requested topic for Sunday School teacher workshops. Discipline problems threaten the volunteer teacher's feeling of success and are therefore one of the issues that makes enlisting new teachers difficult.

But effective discipline is not magic. It does not require a college degree. It is often the result of applied common sense.

Setting

Let's start with one of the basics: setting up the classroom. You can improve order in your teaching experience and avoid many discipline problems simply by setting up your classroom for success.

Step one in solving discipline problems is eliminating them before they happen. Think about these common complaints:

- The first graders in one classroom won't stop playing with toys in the preschool classroom where they meet for Sunday School.

- The preschool teacher loses control of her students before the end of the lesson each week as the students notice their parents waiting outside the door.

- The junior high class starts late each week because the teacher must coax the students away from the pool table in the youth room.

- The high school class is more often a multitude of side conversations between students than a dialogue between the teacher and class.

In each case, there are distractions that lead to poor discipline.

Eliminating Distractions

The easiest answers are not found in tougher application of rules but in the elimination of distractions. Cover the toys (a simple sheet may do; out of sight truly is often out of mind). Orient the preschool teaching area away from the doorway so that waiting parents are not in the students' line of sight. Remove the pool cues and balls from the junior high room before class (or relocate to another space). Conduct the high school class around a table for a few weeks rather than on the youth room couches and pillows (couches and pillows create an environment of informality and undirected activity that is often conducive to youth ministry, but not to education).

Be alert to the environmental factors that get things off course in your classroom, and correct them before the students arrive. Lobby for classroom furnishings that are appropriate for your age group and educational purpose. A few minutes of preparation will be time well spent.

Think About

- My students' biggest distraction in our classroom is . . .

- How can I deal with or eliminate distractions in my classroom?

- If I wanted to relocate my students, where could I take them?

Section2

Preventive Discipline

Behold, blessed is the one whom God reproves; therefore despise not the discipline of the Almighty. For He wounds, but He binds up; He shatters, but His hands heal.

Job 5:17–18

Ten Ways to Prevent Discipline Problems

Tom Nummela

OPENING THOUGHT

Would you rather resolve a discipline problem or prevent one?

Review

As the title suggests, many Sunday School discipline problems are solved more easily by prevention than cure. Teachers are well advised to be proactive in preparing and executing lesson plans. Simple things you can do in advance will greatly affect the behavior of your students.

Consider these ten suggestions as preventative medicine to stave off discipline problems in your classroom:

1. Nothing can beat a good start. The minutes that students are alone in a classroom—or are present with other students or adults who do not perceive themselves to be in charge—are a breeding ground for discipline problems. Head off discipline problems by being in the classroom before the first student arrives, and have a plan for keeping the students who arrive early busy and engaged.

2. While being early is a significant step, it may not be enough. Don't waste your advantage by leaving these precious early minutes to be expended in last-minute preparation—making photocopies, reviewing lesson plans, or engaging in conversation with fellow teachers. These early minutes are excellent opportunities to focus on your students. Provide presession activities that prepare for the lesson of the day. Converse with your students, getting to know their favorite activities.

3. Our names are a significant part of our identity. Knowing your students' names will connect you with them in a most significant way. Use whatever means necessary to learn the names of your students, such as nametags for the students to wear or place near them on the table. Review names fre-

quently, especially in the first lesson or two each quarter and whenever you gain a new student or have a visitor. Address the students by name in class, but also whenever you see them outside the classroom. Such recognition is a powerful indication of your interest in them and their welfare.

4. Knowing names is just a first step. Find a little time each week to find out other things about your students. Perhaps you can have a weekly sharing session (ask about pets, sports involvement, favorite school activities, or vacation plans). Call or visit each student's home for a friendly chat. (How much better it is when the first contact you have with a child's parents is not about a discipline problem!) The stronger the relationship is between you and each of your students, the less likely it is that there will be discipline problems in class.

5. Often, the first question a parent may ask a Sunday School student is, "Who was your teacher today?" It is all too often something that the student doesn't know. When nametags are used, have one of your own. Write your name on the board where it is visible to your students. Introduce yourself at the beginning of class. Send home frequent signed notes for parents, including your phone number or e-mail address. Do whatever it takes to make sure that students and parents know who you are and can contact you if they desire. The calls or visits already mentioned will serve to meet this goal also.

6. A first step to gaining the behavior you desire from your students is to tell them what that behavior is. Establish these rules by fiat or through classroom discussion. Make them reasonable and positive, and limit them to three or four. (Consider simple rules like "Respect each other" and "Only one person talks at a time.") Let your students create or decorate a classroom poster that will keep them fresh in mind.

7. Review your classroom rules with your students regularly, perhaps even weekly. In most Sunday Schools, many children do not attend every week. For some students, a weekly reminder is very helpful. Direct the class's attention to specific rules as suggested by classroom behavior.

8. Having at least two adults present in every classroom every week may be a requirement set by your congregation's liability insurance provider. Even if it is not the case in your church, take it upon yourself to recruit a team teacher, assistant, or even a rotation of parents to be present in the classroom as you teach. Especially if several volunteers rotate into the classroom, prepare a simple list of "Ways You Can Help" for these volunteers (things like distributing materials as the teacher directs, moving close to any student who seems to have difficulty focusing or is bothering another child, escorting a child to the restroom, or leading a simple activity if the teacher has to leave the room for any reason). The goal here is continuous and flexible adult supervision. Two adults in a room more than doubles the sense of security and stability in the classroom.

9. Sometimes, despite your best preparation, an activity you have chosen fails to engage the students or results in more chaos than desired. Be prepared enough, nimble enough, to bring such an activity to a smooth and swift end and move on to something else. Sometimes the activity can be reintroduced in a modified form. Sometimes something else will work as well or better.

10. At times, the behavior of a student may make a teacher angry. But a wise teacher will seek to deal with every child, even one who is being rude or disrespectful, in a calm manner. A raised voice or angry expression will negatively affect all the children in class, not just the one who is misbehaving. In a tense situation, step back mentally and take a deep breath or spend a moment outside the classroom, perhaps in prayer, and assess what will be your best course of action or what assistance you might require.

Not every instance of misbehavior can be avoided, but preparation and planning will go a long way toward keeping your classroom trouble free. When the students are engaged in activities they enjoy and that keep them focused, they are more disciplined disciples. God bless you as you teach His children His Word.

Think About

- One surprise for me in this article is . . .

- If you had to focus on just one of these suggestions, which would it be? Why?

- How could staffing changes affect discipline in your classroom?

- Who else on your Sunday School team could benefit from reading this essay?

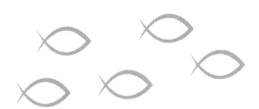

A No-Problem Classroom

Michael Eschelbach

OPENING THOUGHT

What might the author mean by the "space, pace, and face" of discipline?

Review

Many a parent or adult member of a congregation thinks twice before agreeing to teach children because they are afraid. People are afraid, and rightly so, that a classroom full of young people will mean war—a test of wills between teacher and students. Can a well-meaning adult believer win this war? Do we even want to engage this battle for the souls and minds of our children? The answer is a resounding "Yes, with the help of the Lord!" Remember, more than once the Lord provided victory for His people in the Old Testament while they slept, without a single casualty. For more than twenty years, I have been teaching children in the church in a "no problems" classroom. The key is a positive environment that displays the presence of the living God in three particular ways: space, pace, and face.

Space

The physical space is the first way in which we can provide a positive classroom environment for Christian education. The best space for Christian education is the sanctuary. The sanctuary serves well because it has its own impressive voice. This is where we worship, where the Lord meets us through the pastor and through the Word and Sacraments. The sanctuary is bigger than we are, yet it exists for our benefit, to be a "safe place" for us. The sanctuary is full of furnishings, fabrics, and art, all of which help to impress the lessons of God's Word.

Unfortunately, everyone can't meet in the sanctuary for class—but you can make your classroom a sanctuary. Spend some time to make sure the room you use is well cared for (clean, freshly painted, bright) and well appointed with art, maps, or other appointments that remind us of God's presence. If they are able, enlist your students' help to prepare and maintain the room. This will give them a sense of ownership and motivate them to treat the room well.

If possible, begin your class outside the room. Many Sunday Schools have an opening in the sanctuary before going to class. This is a good way to set the tone for what is coming. A common opening also is a good time to make sure everyone knows how we deal with students who are struggling with behavior. If there is no such opening, you might meet the children outside the room and talk about what is to come.

At your opening, remind the students that the presence of the Word of God makes any place a sanctuary. If you do your own opening, start in an available common space (narthex or even outside) with the invocation and a brief prayer (such as the collect for the day) and then enter the room. This is a time to talk about conduct that sets the students up for success in any classroom and any other place. Because they are not in the room yet, students have opportunity to adjust their thinking. If a student has trouble in class, that person will know that your response is still in the interest of his or her success in your class and elsewhere.

During class, take advantage of the space, appointments, and art often. Make notes in your lesson plan so you don't forget! For example, ask the class, "What season of the church year is it? How could you know?" (Look at, or remember, the cloth on the altar, pulpit, and lectern. Its color reveals the season.) "Is there a painting or stained glass window depicting a symbol or Bible story that fits this season or matches our lesson? Was there a particular phrase in a hymn today or part of a text that speaks to our particular lesson?" In all these ways, you may continually raise the students' consciousness of the space they are in. God meets us in this space through all our senses to provide limitless potential for our lives!

Pace

Pace has more to do with the teacher's preparation than with how fast or slowly she or he teaches the content. Children and young people are very discerning. They know if you are nervous and uncomfortable. They know if you are teaching someone else's material or teaching your conviction and the truth it is founded upon. The more I've planned and internalized my lessons, the better I am at adjusting the pace in all kinds of ways for the benefit of the class. Here's how I do it.

I find a lesson worksheet or student page to be essential, but I use only one. Too many papers are a distraction and cause for disorganization. One worksheet on interesting paper (color, watermark, border) with a remarkable format and font provides a picture—a map of where class is going today.

A two-sided single sheet is okay, but a single side is even better. This sheet gives the "high spots" and important reference material for the class. It serves as a guide for both students and teacher, and you should know it thoroughly.

Prepare all materials for each lesson in advance so that there is no interruption to the flow of the lesson to locate or distribute needed materials. Move confidently from one activity to the next so that the students' attention is held and not allowed to wander. This level of advance preparation will allow you to teach with passion and flexibility.

Passion demonstrates that the content is important to you and integral to your life of faith. Let's say the lesson is Daniel and the lions' den. You might begin with feigned anger and malice as you look around at your class and say, "Who does that Daniel think he is?" You move close to one student, point at him, and say, "Do you know this Daniel? Are you a friend of his?" Watch as the students' eyes and expressions follow yours. Do they know about Daniel? If so, they can tell the story to you. If not, you can tell them about him or you can read the story. Or you can act out the story together. Your passionate portrayal of Daniel's enemy will demonstrate that this is not some dull history from a dusty book; Daniel was a real man of faith, facing real threats with a life of faith. Applying the lesson to the real lives of your students (Whom do your students see as enemies? What "dens of lions" do they face?) is easier, and your students will be so bound up in the lesson that they have neither time nor interest in making trouble.

Flexibility is another by-product of preparation. Every lesson will have tangents—questions that the students raise or spontaneous ideas that can touch the students' lives. You should be so well prepared that you can follow the tangent briefly, yet return to the lesson plan without difficulty—or change the lesson plan "on the fly" if the lesson's progress dictates.

Face

Faces of authority in the lives of our students are a third defense against misbehavior in the classroom. Misbehavior is sin, and sin is the result of the continued presence of the sinful nature, even in children of faith. Therefore it is true that the Law, represented by faces of authority, will hold the sinful nature in check. When meeting with my confirmation class, I often required one parent of each child (or sponsor of some kind) to attend also. These parents usually sat in the back, but they were still there.

At other times, I paired every younger student with an older one. These mentors not only help a student stay with the lesson but also eliminate most interruptions or discipline problems before they begin. Older students are eager to be of service in a real way, often explain things so the trailing student can understand, and offer correction or warning about conduct.

In a smaller Sunday School room, only one or two older youth or adults may be available to serve as mentors. Still, these other faces of authority help keep the sinful nature of restless students in check. I have never found these authorities to hinder class; interested students quickly forget peripheral matters. But their presence is significant, and calling attention to them has an immediate effect. These assistants are vital in the event that misbehavior that disrupts the learning of others occurs; they can help implement the agreed-upon discipline steps (talking to the student briefly outside of class or taking the unruly student to the superintendent or his or her parents, perhaps) without the teacher having to interrupt the pace of the class.

The faces of parents, pastor, teachers, and mentors need never express enmity or opposition. Be careful never to threaten your students. Warnings and threats suggest meanness rather than love, and idle threats quickly undercut authority. Simply apply discipline evangelically and immediately. Everyone will benefit. The unruly student learns about consequences, the class can continue with little interruption, and all students receive an object lesson in discipline; they also should see that you act with gentleness.

Love

With attention to space, pace, and face, your witness of love for these children need never be compromised by frustration, anger, or angry words. And your witness to the love of God through His Word will not be compromised by distractions. This is Christian education, and we will all work together wisely, enthusiastically, and lovingly to bring our children along in the faith. Yours will become a "no problems" classroom that wins every war before there is ever a battle.

Think About

- One thing I want to concentrate on is . . .

- How could you modify your space?

- How does your pace affect your learners?

- In what way does my face affect students?

Powerful Presence

Mindy Walz

Review

Remember as a kid how a couple of your peers could be messing around (not you, of course), and the teacher would quietly move right behind the offenders? Suddenly, the misbehavers would feel the teacher's presence, glance up, and quickly correct themselves—doing their best to slink innocently back into the right behavior. That teacher didn't have to have a major confrontation. He or she used the power of proximity instead.

Think about the group or groups you work with most often. If the group is very small, with just a few kids, the power of proximity is an automatic factor. You sit or work in the midst of the group and engage each student individually. If the group is bigger, though, what is your typical style? Do you stay at one spot in the front, or do you move around the group while you are talking or while they are working on an activity?

Going Mobile

Being mobile and being able to notice what is going on in the group isn't always easy. The ability to shift your position without disrupting a group activity is a skill that comes with experience. Start by uprooting yourself from your comfort spot. In a classroom setting, move toward a student you notice fidgeting. Perhaps ask him a question as a part of the lesson to help re-engage him in what is going on (not just to put him on the spot). If groups are working on a craft in VBS and one group is having a hard time staying on task, move to that group and ask what step they are on. Find something good about what they have done, and see if they need help. If you are with preschool children and two or three are paying more attention to each other than the story, get up and sit near those students. Don't miss a beat; carry on with the story where you left off. Sometimes, younger kids may say something such as, "Why did you move?" Just keep your response simple, and get back on task. Say, "I'm sitting here now," and continue with the story. Often, this change gets everyone back on track.

Using the power of proximity will not eliminate the need to deal with all discipline issues directly. If, however, your goal is to create an atmosphere where students are engaged with minimal disruptions, your presence can be the power to deal with small problems that often pop up. As with anything else, the more comfortable you become with using this technique, the more effective it will be.

As you grow in experience, you will find the power of proximity is an effective tool for maintaining discipline. In fact, you may be surprised by the power your presence!

Think About

- This could benefit my teaching by . . .

- How might your students respond to your close proximity?

- How could you become more comfortable with this technique?

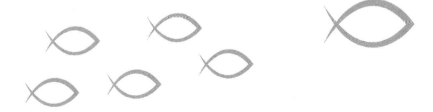

Just Necessary, Not Evil

Mindy Walz

Review

Discipline. It may not sound like much fun, and the word itself may even cause some to feel rebellious. The prospect of it may intimidate and even keep away some adults who are considering work with young people. Others may idealistically argue that in a Christian setting, discipline shouldn't even be necessary. After all, everyone is living as they should and loving others as they ought, right? Still others may argue that maintaining discipline in classes or events at church is too rigid and controlling; they want the kids to be able to have fun and not have to worry about too many rules.

I can assure you, however, that in your position as a teacher (or leader of teachers) in a church setting, establishing and maintaining expectations and boundaries is definitely a necessary thing. While the atmosphere may be—and probably should be—more relaxed than in a school classroom, maintaining order can actually allow everyone to have more fun than if chaos is reigning.

A New Perspective

Consider the perspective of a visiting child: unsure in an unfamiliar setting, nervous about stepping into a place where she knows no one. Would she be more likely to stay if her view from the doorway was of others her age working on an activity while quietly talking and laughing with one another—or if the others were running around the room, shouting and chasing one another?

Providing structure and boundaries actually creates a more welcoming environment. It also creates a setting where more fun can be had by everyone involved. There is also less of a chance that a few children with strong personalities will essentially run the whole group, teachers included. Obviously, different settings—and different groups with different dynamics—call for different approaches. For example, a second-grade Sunday School class calls for a different atmosphere than a middle school youth group game night.

In both cases, however, establishing and maintaining clear expectations is important for a successful learning and growing environment.

A New Atmosphere

So, how can you create the peaceful and welcoming atmosphere that is so important? No one wants to be an ogre, and you shouldn't have to be. Keep in mind, though, that as a teacher or leader of children, you have a position of authority according to Scripture. While it is never right for adults to abuse that position of authority, it also is not right for children to disrespect those who are in authority. Disrespecting those whom God has placed in positions of authority can eventually lead to disrespecting the authority of God as well.

Teachers and leaders need to believe that if they have been placed in charge of a group, it is okay to be in charge. In fact, they have a responsibility to provide firm, loving guidance to those placed in their care. Providing structure and setting clear expectations is not mean; it is loving. Structure and expectations create an atmosphere in which the Gospel can be heard. God promises to bless the sowing of His Word; He will be with you and your class as you teach and learn.

Think About

- Discipline is necessary because . . .

- Why is being in charge okay?

- What is the most important expectation you have for your students?

Rethink Your Routine

Lyla Glaskey

Review

Sunday School teachers sometimes wonder how regular classroom teachers handle discipline day after day, especially after a frustrating or challenging class. Most teachers know that routines can help students feel secure, establish a predictable framework, and lessen discipline problems.

But routines can also contribute to discipline issues if the basic needs of kids are not included in the planning. Take a look at your routine and seating arrangement, and make sure it is helping, not hurting, your classroom discipline.

First

You know that kids bring a lot more with them to Sunday School than just shiny quarters for the offering basket. Kids often bring a bad case of the crankies because they were up late on Saturday night, and they're hungry because they rushed out of the house without breakfast. Consider a routine snack. Adults often underestimate the difference it can make in a child's behavior.

Next

Make sure your routine allows you to accomplish what is really important. Sometimes teachers feel they must follow the Sunday School curriculum's set routine to the letter. Try treating the lesson plan more like a menu and less like a recipe. If you see red flags the instant you read an activity suggested for the lesson, follow that instinct! Find an alternative that will work for your students. Set a routine that protects the most important elements of the lesson, but give yourself the permission and flexibility to make the lesson work for you.

Last

If you are having discipline challenges, look at your seating arrangement. Just as in real estate, location, location, location matters in discipline. Classroom teachers know that changing a kid's location often changes the kid's behavior. Seating charts are harder to determine in Sunday School, as attendance may vary from week to week, but you can have a general idea in mind of where you want certain children placed. The child that derails class with constant or off-topic questions may be better off in the back corner. The quiet child may feel better up close to the teacher, where soft answers can be heard. Set a buffer of a few compliant children between two contentious students. Don't hesitate to quietly move kids during the lesson if needed. Try to have a spot somewhere in the room where a child can go until he or she can handle being part of the class. Even better, partner with another teacher, and send disruptive children to another room for a while. Removing the audience often subdues the problem. Make sure students know they are welcome back as soon as they can handle themselves appropriately.

The fact that it is Sunday School doesn't mean you can't use a few tricks out of the regular classroom teachers' book. Sunday School is important, and it's okay to shape the routine more like that of a regular classroom if needed.

Think About

- The most important part of my classroom routine is . . .

- What attitudes are my students bringing to class with them?

- How could my routine change to affect students positively?

Got To or Get To?

David Ebeling

Review

By transitioning from "got tos" to "get tos," discipline issues will actually decrease because the children get more excitement out of being there.

Ask any child. At a very early age, they will know the difference between "got tos" and "get tos." Attitudinally, there is a world of difference. "I've got to do it" has a negative connotation. However, when children are talking about something they highly desire or want to do, you may hear them say, "I get to do it."

A "got to" is a requirement, a must-do, a no-choice command.

A "get to" is a privilege, a choice, an alternative that is desired by the learners.

In Sunday School, there certainly are some got tos. Children are to pay attention, to keep their hands to themselves, to follow the teacher's lead, and to participate in the activities that take place during the class period. Those are the basics. We certainly hope, though, that there will also be a number of get tos.

As the Sunday School teacher, you control the number and conditions of the get tos. It may seem easier to teach using mostly got tos and fewer get tos. When everyone is assigned the same thing throughout the entire class period, there is less commotion and chaos. But the wise teacher knows that learners love the independence when allowed to make choices. By transitioning from got tos to get tos, discipline issues will actually decrease because the children get more excitement out of being there. They get choices. They are more motivated.

Example 1:

Got to: Have the learners read the Bible narrative, taking turns reading. Each child must read one Bible verse in sequence around the table.

Get to: Turn the Bible narrative into a simple drama. Let the children choose a part or opt to be a helper in some other way, such as controlling a light switch or turning the CD off and on for background music or sound effects.

Example 2:

Got to: Everyone is assigned the same memory verse.

Get to: Introduce and read several verses; children may choose one to memorize. Or, let them pick an appropriate verse; a motivated student will invest considerable time searching the Scriptures for just the right one. In addition, you can let them choose a way to demonstrate their success, such as saying the verse for the teacher before or after class, writing it out with an illustration, or completing a puzzle based on the verse.

Yes, there must be got tos in your class. But when you plan at least one get to for each class period, the learners will most likely be more attentive and less disruptive.

Think About

- Got tos are easier, but . . .
- Outline two got tos changed into get tos.

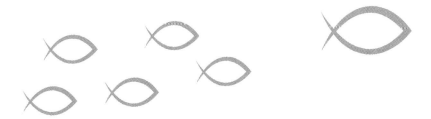

Attitude Check

Dave Ebeling

Review

It's time for an attitude check! Discipline in the classroom starts with the teacher's attitude, whether negative or positive. With a negative attitude, learning is hindered and discipline problems may increase. With a positive attitude, fewer discipline problems will arise.

Preparation

Negative Attitude: "It's Saturday night. I'm glad I know that story. I can wing it."

Positive Attitude: "I'll check the main idea of next week's lesson on Sunday so I can ponder, pray, and plan all week."

Start planning your lesson early in the week. Have your materials ready. Make a new craft, learn that song, or study the context of the Bible narrative. Predetermine seating, perhaps using folded paper tents to identify students. Be present to greet the first student to arrive. Start on time. When learners see you are prepared, discipline problems are reduced.

Management

Negative Attitude: "I'd better let the kids have fun so they'll come back."

Positive Attitude: "I'll manage my class well so we all get the most out of every minute together."

Be firm. Give clear directions. Demonstrate how you want things done. Establish simple, consistent rules. Anticipate distractions. Refocus with positive touch or talk. When the children are confident in your management style, discipline problems are reduced.

Techniques

Negative Attitude: "They're supposed to sit and listen to me."

Positive Attitude: "I'll make the class so interesting that the kids will wonder where the time went."

Plan the class time with four or five age-appropriate activities. Verbally direct smooth transitions from one to the next. Involve the children in reading or dramatizing the story. Sing. Give learners natural opportunities to refocus throughout the class time. When students are focused, discipline problems are reduced.

Relationships

Negative Attitude: "I'm glad I have these kids just one hour a week."

Positive Attitude: "I want to learn about each child."

Talk to students when they arrive. Listen to what's happening in their lives. Know something each likes to do away from church. Pray with and for your learners. When children know you care about them personally, discipline problems are reduced.

Parents

Negative Attitude: "No wonder these kids are a problem in class. Look at their parents."

Positive Attitude: "What an awesome opportunity it is to partner with parents and help their children grow in Christ."

Talk to the parents. Learn their names. Ask for their input if you are unsure of how to handle a situation that involves their child. Commend their children's positive behavior and contributions to the class. Encourage and prepare them to talk about God's love at home. When parents accept you as a partner, discipline problems are reduced.

Think About

- A negative attitude I have . . .
- Which attitude area would you work on first?
- Outline a plan for each of the attitude areas in your classroom.

Rules of the Room

Tom Nummela

Review

I travel quite a bit by car. I consider it a relatively safe way to travel. Auto accidents occur to only a very small number of the millions of vehicles that travel our roadways each day. The rules of the road—the state traffic law—that govern those who drive, and our obedience to them, turn potential chaos into orderly transportation.

Your Sunday School classroom can also benefit from rules. A few simple rules, and your students' obedience to them, can tame a potentially wild group of children and allow you to do what you came for—teaching the Gospel. Here are some tips for making it work for you.

1. **Start right away.** The best time to establish some "rules of the room" is on your first day with this group of students.

2. **Involve the students in determining the rules.** Many of your students will be familiar with this process from their public or Day School experiences.

3. **You make the final list.** Incorporate your students' suggestions as you are able, but don't abdicate your responsibility as teacher.

4. **Usually three or four rules will do.** "One person talks at a time; the others listen. Get permission before leaving your seat. Treat others with respect." Your list may be very different, since each group seems to have different bad habits.

5. **Post the rules in a prominent place.** Review them as needed. Revise them when necessary.

6. **Enforce the rules consistently, fairly, and without anger.** "Anna, our classroom rule is only one person talks at a time. Right now, that's me." Often simply pointing to a rule where it is posted will be enough to restrain offenders.

7. **Compliment those who follow the rules.** Catch your students being good. As often as possible, comment on the good behavior of the whole class.

8. **Freely forgive those who break the rules.** Demonstrate your love for them in Christ, and tell them of Christ's love for them. God really does love sinners. Aren't we glad?

9. **Think carefully before establishing a system of rewards or punishments.** Children often obey rules "just because." They appreciate an orderly classroom experience as much as you do.

If you choose to reward, keep it simple. Plan your class so that orderly participation results in the reward of enjoyable activity. Consider concluding the lesson with a period of review using enjoyable games. When students behave, the time for fun is longer at the end. Yes, rules are a form of Law. They restrain unruly behavior. They also establish an atmosphere where the Gospel can be spoken and heard.

Think About

- Good rules help us because . . .

- Which rules are essential for your classroom?

- Write out four or five rules that you must have in your classroom.

Section 3

Managing Classroom Discipline

At the end of your life you groan, when your flesh and body are consumed, and you say, "How I hated discipline, and my heart despised reproof! I did not listen to the voice of my teachers or incline my ear to my instructors. I am at the brink of utter ruin in the assembled congregation."

Proverbs 5:11–14

What Works: Classroom Discipline

Jane Fryar

Review

How did you learn to teach Sunday School? Most of us learned by watching other teachers. We remember our third-grade Sunday School teacher helping us act out Bible stories, so we find a way to have our third graders do it. We recall our youth leader bringing doughnuts every week, so we stop at the doughnut shop on our way to class.

Using the methods we have seen working well has legitimacy. It even has a name: "action research." We notice what works for us or for others and incorporate it into our teaching repertoire. Until 1970 or so, "teaching as we were taught" and using "action research" were just about the only way to go—for volunteer and professional teachers.

What Works

The decade of the seventies, though, marked the beginning of an explosion in scientific research focused on answering the question, "What works in classrooms?" The research continues today, more vigorously than ever. But the dust of the initial explosion has started to settle. By putting many similar studies side by side and noting conclusions in a process known as meta-analysis, researchers have shown that certain approaches make a real difference. We don't have all the answers, but we do have some!

As God's children, we see these answers as a gift from our Creator! As Martin Luther explained the First Article of the Apostles' Creed, he noted that our Lord has given "eyes, ears, and all my members, my reason and all my senses." Eyes that see, ears that hear, and minds that reason make it possible to explore our world, to use the knowledge God has given in ways that honor Him.

What better way to do that than in teaching God's redeemed, baptized people to know and love Him more and more?

On Task

It only makes good sense. Students who focus on the topic at hand learn more than those who fail to focus. Educators call this "time on task." In some classrooms, so many disruptions occur that students spend only 21 percent of their time on task! In the best classrooms, researchers have shown that students spend more than 70 percent of their time on task. Guess who learns more!

Think about it. How much time does your class spend "on task"? Want to know? Have a friend sit in the back of your room with a sheet of paper and a list of numerals from one to fifty—assuming your class session is fifty minutes long. Your partner should put a *Y* (yes) or an *N* (no) next to each numeral in answer to the question, is the class focused on learning now? Then plug the data into this formula:

Number of yeses divided by total number of minutes available × 100 = % time on task

Would you like to increase the learning that goes on in your Sunday School class? Research points to four key "best practices" you can use.

Routines

Think first in terms of routine classroom events and the needs of your students. Ask yourself questions like these:

How quickly do you get into the lesson? What keeps you from beginning the moment the clock strikes nine? Do you prepare materials before class? Could students help you rearrange chairs or tables before class if rearranging is necessary? What incentive could you offer to encourage everyone to arrive a few minutes early?

How could you distribute materials more efficiently? Could learners pick up Bibles, pencils, and snacks as they arrive? What other routines would help you?

What events consistently disrupt learning? Does a bell ring midway through class? Who could help prevent that? Do specific students ask every week to use the restroom? How could you create a process for dismissing them that would keep them safe while not interrupting your train of thought?

Rules

Now consider classroom rules. Do students know what you expect? Experts suggest these approaches:

Let class members help you set rules. Accept ideas and suggestions, but make it clear that as the adult in the room, you have final responsibility and, thus, authority.

Limit rules in number. Then make sure everyone understands both the "what" and the "why" behind each rule. Post a list. If you share a space, put the rules on a poster and bring it back each week.

Attach clear and appropriate rewards and consequences to each rule. Remember, rules that are unenforced become unenforceable.

With It

"With-it-ness" is that sixth sense, the "eyes in the back of a teacher's head." Even while we focus on E.J.'s question, we notice Jill is fidgeting and Madeline looks sleepy. And—here's the key—we act on what we see to prevent problems. We move to stand beside Jill. We ask Madeline a question. We propose a contest to draw everyone's attention back to the topic at hand.

This, of course, means arranging furniture to make it possible. If you share a space, be creative! Think about how to enact a four-by-four approach—moving to within four feet of each learner every four minutes.

Effective procedures combined with teacher "with-it-ness" will prevent many disruptions, and prevention is your goal. But disruptions will occur in even the best classrooms. When you notice an issue developing, address it immediately! Students who have collaborated in developing rules and who have seen you enforce them with firm, caring consistency will generally respond to a simple, quiet reminder.

Remember, most rule breaking is not intended as an insult. Usually, disruptive children have been distracted. Or they are hungry. Or they haven't fully engaged the concept you're communicating. Teachers who avoid personalizing disruptive behavior can deal more effectively with it. Address the underlying problem, and the disruption disappears. The other articles in this issue offer a multitude of suggestions for tackling specific discipline issues.

Care

We've saved the most important point for last. When, in Christ, we care about our students, they know it. They respond, in turn, by loving us in the Savior too. Care is never a "group policy." One by one, child by child, we notice new shoes, we pray for ailing grandparents, we phone or e-mail to ask about that geometry test.

In maintaining a well-managed classroom, we make learning possible. But even more importantly, we model Jesus' concern and His love for our students.

Think About

- A classroom discipline plan provides . . .

- What discipline focus is most important for your classroom?

- How "on task" are your students? How could you improve their on-task time?

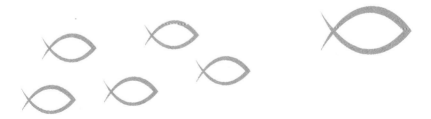

The Proximity Advantage

David Ebeling

Review

Proximity refers to distance. In a learning environment, proximity is the physical distance between you (the teacher) and each individual learner. Maintaining discipline and positive class control is affected by how you vary that distance by moving around.

Some children want you close by; others are more comfortable as far from you as possible. Some children find it difficult to focus on learning, so you move near them—even close enough to place your hand on the child's shoulder. Some are so shy that if you move near them, it triggers excessive anxiety. As the teacher, you must know your children well enough to make that judgment.

Your Setting

At one church, four Sunday School classes share a large room, one assigned to each corner. During the week, that large room is used for preschool classes, so furniture, toys, and equipment—covered with sheets—are lining the walls. This setting is not unusual for Sunday School. Many churches have to subdivide rooms, using portable bulletin boards or sliding dividers to capture some privacy for the teacher and his or her learners. Often, it is so cramped that it is difficult to move about in the limited space allowed.

If you teach in one of these tight spaces, you could sit down and never move out of your chair. It might seem easier to teach this way because there is not much space to physically maneuver. Yet, by moving around the space you do have, you claim the proximity advantage. By glancing at children's work from different angles, intentionally changing the distance between you and your learners, and alternating between sitting and standing, you employ the advantages of classroom proximity.

Whether your classroom space is tight or sufficient, when you alter the distances between you and the learners by moving around, their senses are activated.

As you walk from one side of the classroom to the other, your learners' eyes move with your movements and they see you from various angles. Your learners listen more attentively because your sound waves are approaching their ears from different directions. When you brush against the arm of a learner or gently touch a shoulder, you activate their feelings. Even the sense of smell might be triggered if you are wearing a scent that can be noticed.

Move about in your classroom. Vary the distance between you and your learners. Activate your children's senses.

Think About

- The space I teach in is . . .

- How could you adapt your class meeting space to encourage learning?

- How does your classroom affect your students' discipline?

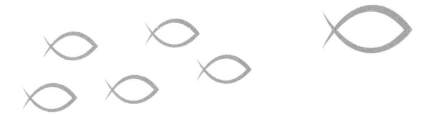

Managing Classroom Behavior

Tom Nummela

Review

Teaching a class of fifteen active third graders? Worried about things getting out of hand? Think of it as a social function you arrange for fifteen people. Teachers don't need a magic formula or a secret weapon to get good behavior in class. You can use the same skills and techniques you might employ in a social situation—planning, creating a pleasant atmosphere, attending to the relationships in the group, and dealing with the unexpected.

Planning

A good experience in the classroom is determined in large degree by what the teacher does before class. Just as you wouldn't try to entertain guests without planning ahead—determining the setting, menu, entertainment, activities, and such—the teacher who enters the classroom without adequate preparation is probably inviting undesirable behavior.

When a lesson is well planned, the students' attention is captured and held, the teacher is respected and appreciated, the lesson flows, the teacher can recover quickly from tangents, and the needs of the individual children can be met. Advance preparation will head off most discipline problems.

Atmosphere

When you entertain at home, you give attention to the setting. You may decorate around a special theme to "draw your guests in." You will certainly eliminate annoying distractions (putting away the ongoing craft project, turning down the stereo, putting the cat in the garage). You'll do the best you can to make your guests comfortable in your home.

In class, the same attention is required. Are there toys in the room that will distract the kindergartners you teach? You may need to find closed storage or even relocate your class to eliminate the distraction. Are your junior high students getting "too comfortable"—sitting on the tables or getting into cupboards where they don't have any business? You may need to remind them that they are guests. Set and enforce limits.

Relationships

A good host teacher will be present to welcome the guests when they arrive, to make them comfortable, to introduce them if necessary, and to get them involved in the gathering. These simple steps will further reduce inappropriate behavior.

Knowing your students is another key. As you demonstrate your interest in the students, listen to them, affirm them, share Christ's unconditional love with them, and enjoy them, they will respond accordingly. Build relationships through activities each week that help the students share their personal histories and interests, create interaction, and allow students to work together toward common goals.

The Unexpected

No social experience will run perfectly. But not every glitch will ruin the day. Some unexpected problems can be addressed in the classroom by switching to an alternate activity or simply skipping ahead to the next activity. Some minor misbehavior can be ignored. Some can be pointed out without fanfare, consequences mentioned if necessary, and the class can proceed.

Occasionally, student misbehavior will be serious enough to warrant interrupting class and stopping the behavior or removing a student.

Dealing with the unexpected also falls in the area of advance preparation. The teacher needs to decide in advance on alternate lesson activities, behaviors that can be ignored, and procedures for disciplining or removing unruly students.

With advance preparation, attention to atmosphere and relationships, and anticipation of problems, you may find that teaching is a lot more like entertaining friends than you thought.

Think About

- My role as host should include . . .

- What cues could you give students as guests in your classroom?

- How could the host/guest model help with your classroom management?

It's All in How You Say It

Lyla Glaskey

OPENING THOUGHT

Think of a recent situation influenced by *how* something was said

Review

How you say something can be just as powerful as *what* you say. Have you ever wondered why some children are cooperative for some adults but less cooperative for others? There can be a variety of reasons for this, but one significant factor involves the way the adult speaks to the child.

This is especially true if there are strong-willed students in the group. While strong-willed children often grow into strong leaders, they sometimes present challenges in the classroom. For volunteer Sunday School teachers, an hour with a strong-willed child might prove especially challenging. You may not be able to change the strong-willed child, but you can develop skills to make it easier to work with him or her.

One way to ease the tension and avoid discipline problems is to adjust the way you address the class and give instructions. Changing the way you speak can help you avoid power struggles that bog down your teaching and waste valuable class time.

What You Can Do

First, recognize that you cannot make any child do what you want him or her to do. What you can do is increase the chances that her or she will want to do what you ask. People who try to "make children behave" need to take a second look at Genesis—even the perfect Father did not force His children to obey Him. By building positive relationships with our students, we increase their desire to please us and do as we ask.

Next, try using "I" instead of "you." For example, instead of "Turn to page 15," try "I'm starting on page 15; who wants to read with me?" Substitute "Be quiet, or there will be no snack!" with "I pass out snacks to students who are quiet." Try replacing "Stop talking when it's not your turn!" with "I listen to students who raise their hands."

Don't all those phrases mean the same thing? Yes, but the big difference is the avoidance of the power struggle. For some children, the unspoken "you" that begins every command comes across as a challenge. Even though a power struggle is not your intention, you have invited one. By focusing your language on what you are going to do, you raise the odds that even those difficult kids will join you. You are able to model how a calm, responsible adult behaves because you are focused on what you are going to do.

Take the time to get to know your strong-willed students. These are the kids who will stand up to peer pressure, refuse to stand by while some injustice takes place, and be strong enough to change the world. It's important that their faith teachers understand them.

Think About

- Verbal messages . . .

- Why do "I" statements better communicate with students than "you" statements?

- Why is knowing your students' traits and habits important?

- What are some "you" statements you could change to "I" statements with your students?

The Power of Stress

David Ebeling

OPENING THOUGHT

What level of stress do you thir is ideal for your classroom?

Review

Q: Should Sunday School be stressful?

A: No, it should not be stressful for the teacher. Yes, it should be stressful for the learners.

While most of us think of a stressful situation as a negative, there must be stress in your classroom if there is going to be learning. Each child has a comfort zone, where stress is absent and the child senses that he or she doesn't have to do much (and therefore really doesn't have to pay attention). The teacher creates stress by inviting learners to move out of their comfort zone, to apply themselves to the task of learning.

The challenge is that the comfort zone for each learner is different and unique. So, the first step is to know your learners well enough to know when they are comfortable and at what point they can and should be pushed just a bit.

Appropriate Stress

For example, Lara is a good reader but very shy. Asking her to read a verse from the Bible would put stress on her, but you know that if you don't ask, she'll never volunteer. So you set her up for success by privately asking her before class if she'd be ready to read that verse when you ask. Yes, you are applying stress, but an appropriate amount with the goal of equipping Lara to read out loud in class.

When we put no stress or very little stress on learners to learn and achieve, they get lazy, apathetic, and easily distracted because they are bored. Adam, the class clown, will be a constant distraction for the rest of the class if you don't challenge him to learn a memory verse, play a role in a skit, or play the bells to accompany the song. One of those "stressors" challenges him to be productive rather than distractive. Discipline problems are lessened.

Inappropriate Stress

When we put too much stress on learners, they get anxious or fearful and are easily distracted because their anxiety overwhelms them. Matthew struggles with focus, so learning all the words of a new song frightens him to the extent that he acts up, gets in trouble, or perhaps even refuses to sing. The stress to memorize is too distracting, leading to a different kind of discipline problem for you.

So, think of your class as a violin. Each string can be individually tuned. With too little stress, the string will not sound at all. With too much, it can break. With the right amount of stress, though, that violin can produce beautiful music. When you know your learners well, you get a sense of the amount of pressure or stress you can apply to each one to keep them productively learning in your classroom. You'll experience less stressful teaching because you've increased the chances that your learners will be neither apathetic nor anxious.

Think About

- Stressors that affect me include . . .

- What is the connection between stress and behavior?

- Is there a place for stress in Sunday School?

- Which of your students would benefit from a little less stress? Which would benefit from a little more?

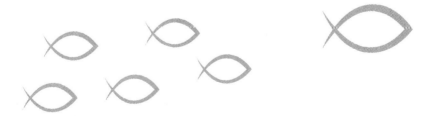

Worth the Risk

David Ebeling

OPENING THOUGHT

True or false? "Variety is the spice of life."

Review

Variety is the spice of life, or so the saying goes. There is life without variety, of course—safe, familiar, and risk free. But variety is often an ingredient that causes growth and learning to take place.

On the other hand, too much variety frightens some learners. Children often value a routine they can count on. A little variety, however, sprinkled among the expectations and familiar patterns of your class routine, will keep the learners on their toes and challenge their brains to think in different ways. Variety can be a major help in maintaining good discipline because it decreases the boredom that can lead to acting out.

Here are several techniques you might try.

Video Clips: If you have a little technical knowledge and the necessary equipment in your classroom, you can show YouTube clips that fit in with the theme and lesson of the day and that are appropriate for your age group. Parents of your students or fellow teachers might even suggest some links if they know you have an interest. Preview them first.

Words on the Wall: Kids love to write and then post their words on the wall. For example, as part of an Easter lesson, you might brainstorm a list of people who saw Jesus alive. Then direct your learners to choose one that they most would like to have been. Have them write their choice on a self-adhesive note and put them all on the wall for others to see.

Rearrange the Room: If your class space allows for it, surprise the children with a new arrangement for tables and chairs one Sunday. The new arrangement could include name tents that specify assigned seating. You can control some discipline issues by putting space between those who often distract each other.

Drama: When teaching the story, identify children to portray various people in the account. Hang homemade nametags around their necks so the class knows whom they are portraying. As you tell the story, help the actors make simple moves or expressions to help the story come alive.

Grab their attention when they least expect it by doing something new from time to time. Variety can be helpful. It's definitely worth the risk.

Think About

- I could grab my students' attention by . . .

- What techniques do you use now that work well?

- Which of the four techniques for variety would you try first?

- What are some other techniques you could try?

Seeking Balance

Dee Christopher

OPENING THOUGHT

How much time each week do you want to spend dealing with behavior problems? Why?

Review

For some, the idea of dealing with discipline in the Sunday School setting is an uncomfortable one. As a volunteer, you may not be trained for classroom management or see it as the reason you became a Sunday School teacher. You have just one hour a week to teach your students, and you want the emphasis to be on hearing the Gospel message, acquiring biblical knowledge, and creating a positive Christian atmosphere in your classroom—not focusing on behavioral issues.

For others, classroom management may be essential as you head into your Sunday School classroom. You desire a well-ordered environment. You think that if you set the rules and students know the consequences for breaking the rules, then you can get on with the purpose of teaching and sharing the Good News of Jesus with your students—not worrying about behavior issues.

Finding Balance

These approaches are not uncommon, and both of them can find a place in a healthy Sunday School classroom. But how do you get there? How do you find a balance between an open approach and an ordered approach? How do you employ the balance of Law and Gospel in the learning setting with students and a volunteer instructor?

You can begin with clear expectations. Call them classroom rules, a classroom covenant, or boundaries. Whatever title you give them, they should be short, clear, reasonable, and easily understood by the children in your classroom.

Positive routines in a welcoming environment lead to a comfortable environment. Follow a basic schedule for each Sunday-morning class. Set a routine and stick to it, but allow for flexibility when the students show they can follow the pattern. A set routine will give students a sense of security, a knowledge of what comes next, and predictability.

Issues Happen

If and when a discipline issue occurs, deal with it in an open, direct manner. This accomplishes more than order in the classroom. It teaches students self-control. Take time to talk with the offender individually. Disciplining in front of the entire class and making an example out of students is not the best approach. Help students recognize what has taken place and how it has hurt the other person, the class, and themselves. Guide students to repent for what they have done wrong and say they are sorry for their behavior. Then let them hear words of forgiveness. Sometimes this process occurs just between teacher and student. Other times, the teacher needs to facilitate this process between students. The sooner you complete this process following the incident, the more effective the results become.

Good communication between yourself and parents also helps tremendously. Get to know the parents of your students so that when issues related to behavior and discipline surface, you can easily communicate and inform the parents concerning what has taken place. This encourages their support in the home for what takes place in the Sunday School classroom.

Above all else, help students see your love for the Lord and your care for them. Let the light of Christ shine through you to them.

Think About

- Next Sunday I will . . .

- What role does routine play in the classroom?

- How should you deal with challenging students?

- What are some clear expectations you can give to the students?

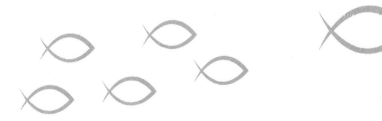

Simple Management Makeovers

Rebecca Fisher

Review

As a professor of education, I see a lot of teachers teaching. Every now and then, I see an idea that helps students focus on the lesson. Try one of these classroom management makeovers the next time you need more order and focus in the classroom so that learning can occur.

Try This

Some children learn early to depend on nonverbal data and touch, rather than written or spoken word. In the casual seating arrangements in Sunday School, their touch can be irritating to neighboring students.

Give each child a lump of Silly Putty for the lesson with this instruction: as long as the putty remains in their hands, they may use it for tactile relief. For some kids, this is both relaxing and critical to their focus. I've seen it work with first graders and with college students!

Are your students restless? At a transition point in the lesson, call out, "Touch two walls."

Students jump up, touch any two walls, one after the other, and then either return to their seats or go to a different place in the room. They're moving and stretching. It makes a difference in their ability to sit through the next section of the lesson.

Do your students have a need to talk? Do they splatter their chatter? Use this social ability, but channel it productively. Pose a situation or question, and give each student a minute to consider a response quietly, individually. Next, have them pair quickly with another child and talk about their conclusions. Then, bring the whole group together for a time to share.

Parents are often the experts at managing their children. Consider sending them a letter introducing yourself and offering this assignment: "In a million words or less, tell me about your child." Parents who take the time to write will give you a treasure trove of ideas for helping the child grow, as well as hints about what works best to motivate and encourage the child.

My own favorite technique comes from a master teacher. When you have a concern about a certain student, spend a few minutes before class sitting in that child's chair, praying for him or her. Ask God for new insight into the student and the knowledge and energy to meet his or her needs as you teach. You and that student will both benefit.

Five simple ideas—put them to work in your classroom for a quick behavior management makeover.

Think About

- One quick makeover I want to try is . . .
- Which of your students will you pray for this week?

The Power of Routine

Rebecca Fisher

OPENING THOUGHT

When was your routine recently disrupted by something unexpected? How did you react?

Review

You walk into church and find your pew is taken. You reach for your toothbrush but come up empty-handed because your daughter has borrowed it for a My Little Pony comb. When routine is interrupted, internal disequilibrium results.

Routine

This certainly holds true for our Sunday School classrooms. Predictable routines are the sinews that hold a classroom together. The more routine a child experiences, the safer the child feels. If you have children of your own, this is clear as crystal because you see the chaos that occurs when that naptime, mealtime, or bedtime routine is interrupted. Routines are even more important in Sunday School because it happens only once a week. Well-crafted routines reduce uncertainty, they are welcoming to new students, and they smooth the waters during your time together.

Another beautiful result of well-crafted routines is a dramatic reduction of discipline issues. When kids know what they are to do, and when and how they are to do it, they generally will fall in line. It's the gray areas that draw the disciplinary challenges.

Thoughtful Attention

Give thoughtful attention to routines for your classrooms. Routine and ritual are part of the rhythm of life; they move us from one point to another. Ask yourself these questions:

- Do I greet my children the same way each Sunday?
- Can I be found in the same place at the same time as they come in?
- Do they know what to do when they arrive to get themselves settled in?
- Do I have a consistent rhythm to the activities of each lesson?

- Are the supplies always found in the same place?

- Are children clear on the type of responses I want them to make when I ask a question?

- Then, when the lesson is finished, do I send them out in a consistent way?

Talk with other Sunday School teachers about the routines they use in their classrooms; beg, borrow, and steal great ideas. Look to excellent Day School teachers for suggestions; their school day is peppered with routine. If you are in a team-teaching situation, it's wise to discuss routines fully with your team teachers so that the students will have that consistency no matter who is teaching that week.

Does implementing more routine mean that your classroom will be stodgy, sit-in-your-seat-and-don't-move rigid? Not at all! Routine is not the enemy of enthusiasm. When the predictable environment you orchestrated allows kids to feel safe, they are free to bloom and grow, to absorb what is being shared, and to be reached deeply by God's Word.

Think About

- One important routine I currently follow is . . .

- Why is predictability important for children?

- Whom could you use as a resource in developing your routine?

- What fun, creative routine can you incorporate in your classroom?

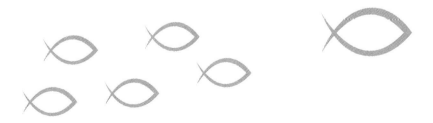

Be Present

Tom Nummela

Review

OPENING THOUGHT

Ten minutes before I teach a Sunday School class, I am usually . . .

It's a simple fact: children find less mischief when the teacher is present than when they are in a classroom without an adult present. The most basic tool for managing classroom behavior is to be in the classroom when the children are there.

Early Arrival

You've committed yourself to the task of teaching Sunday School. For your sake and for the benefit of the children, also commit yourself to arriving in the classroom before your students. It may mean fifteen minutes less sleep, less time with friends after the worship service, or organizing your Sunday-morning routine. But the benefits will be worth it.

- You may have a few minutes to yourself to review your lesson or arrange supplies.

- You can greet each student as he or she arrives. Make each one feel special and welcome.

- You can invite the early students to assist you in preparing the classroom.

- You can get your early arrivals involved in presession activities.

Check your teacher guide for suggestions or for preparation that can be done by the students.

These simple steps will establish a controlled classroom environment that will give you a head start on a productive lesson.

Focused Attention

While you may have a few moments alone in the classroom for preparation and review, once the students arrive, give them your full attention. Prepare your lesson and assemble the necessary supplies and materials in advance, before students arrive in the room. Then you won't have to leave students unattended while you hunt for glue, and you will be able to engage the students from the very first moment they are in class, building relationships and avoiding an activity vacuum that might be filled with misbehavior. Don't leave critical preparations to be done in these few precious moments before class. Prepare necessary photocopies well in advance.

Two Deep

It is immensely easier for a teacher to be always present in the classroom with the students when there are two teachers sharing the classroom duty. Two-deep coverage allows for the occasional brief absences that are often required—delivering the attendance report to the office, monitoring a student's restroom break, or obtaining a missing craft item from the storeroom. It also doubles the one-on-one contact the teachers can have with the children each week. The good news is that it is far easier to recruit the second teacher in each classroom than the first.

Think About

- Ten minutes before class begins, I want to be . . .

- How could students help with classroom preparations?

- What would it take to provide continuous adult presence in your classroom before and during class?

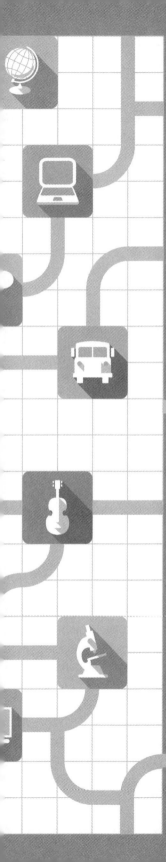

Section 4

Discipline
and Relationships

Have you forgotten the exhortation that addresses you as sons?

"My son, do not regard lightly the discipline of the Lord, nor be weary when reproved by Him. For the Lord disciplines the one He loves, and chastises every son whom He receives."

It is for discipline that you have to endure. God is treating you as sons. For what son is there whom his father does not discipline? If you are left without discipline, in which all have participated, then you are illegitimate children and not sons. Besides this, we have had earthly fathers who disciplined us and we respected them. Shall we not much more be subject to the Father of spirits and live? For they disciplined us for a short time as it seemed best to them, but He disciplines us for our good, that we may share His holiness. For the moment all discipline seems painful rather than pleasant, but later it yields the peaceful fruit of righteousness to those who have been trained by it.

Hebrews 12:5–11

Disciplined Disciples

Jeffrey E. Burkart

OPENING THOUGHT

What is the connection betwee[n] having disciplined students and making disciples?

Review

Discipline and *disciple* have a common origin in the Latin *discipulus* (pupil) and *discere* (to learn). Disciples adhere to the teachings of their master and teach others what the master has taught them.

Discipline also deals with teaching and learning. Unfortunately, it is often equated only with punishment that's meant to change or "train" students to behave in a certain way. Physical punishment was once a common form of discipline. Sometimes punishment takes the form of threats or verbal abuse. Punishment can also take a psychological form such as ignoring others to "teach them a lesson."

Beyond Punishment

But good discipline techniques can go beyond punishment. Let's explore other ways of helping children be disciplined disciples.

Three relationships form an important base for developing disciplined disciples. First, establish a strong relationship with the child. Next, cultivate a relationship with the parents. Finally, help families develop a closer relationship with God. Find out all you can about the children you are teaching. Get to know them and their parents as well as you can. Make a home visit or invite parents to visit you for a few minutes after class to get some insights into the spiritual life of the family.

Knowing the child's family background will help you discover the most appropriate ways to lead the child in Christian discipleship. In addition, when discipline problems occur, having a good relationship with the parents can help solve the problem.

Accentuate the Positive

Express your expectations of children in positive terms—avoid using *don't*. When you tell children what you expect, teach them why you have the expectation. For example: "Listen carefully to what others have to say. Why?

Because we learn from listening to others."

Practice appropriate behaviors with students. This teaches discipline by giving children time to think about their actions and apply what they learn to similar situations. Practice appropriate ways to disagree with someone's point of view, leave when class is dismissed, clean up the classroom, listen, share, and take turns.

Analyze who is giving you "the problem." Sometimes we think that the whole class is giving us a problem when only one or two children are at fault. Avoid holding the whole class responsible for the actions of one person. Martin Luther reminded us that we are all saints and sinners at the same time. We all need God's forgiveness.

Deal swiftly with discipline problems, but watch what you say. Don't blow up at minor disturbances. Avoid moralizing: "Good Christians don't behave like that." To be disciplined disciples, children need to learn that they live under the loving forgiveness of God. At the same time, children also need to learn that living under God's forgiveness doesn't mean they are given a license to sin.

Lavish Praise

Finally, be lavish with praise. Thank children when they are working hard, paying attention, and contributing to the class. Send thank-you cards to children to express your appreciation for something they have done. When we give thanks and praise children, we teach them how to give thanks to and praise each other. Take time to pray for each of your students. Ask God for wisdom to lead them to learn about Him and to be willing to proclaim the Good News of salvation to others.

Think About

- Knowing your disciples means . . .

- Why is it necessary to figure out who is causing problems?

- What role does praise play in discipline?

- How might I build a great relationship with my students? their parents?

Discipline or Discipling?

Martha Streufert Jander

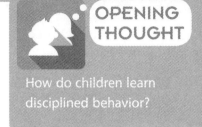
Review

All parents share these concerns for their children: How do we discipline without breaking a child's spirit? How do we "discipline" a child to follow the Savior? Here are several ways.

Jesus is the best example to follow in our lives, but He is much more! He grants faith, forgiveness, new life, and salvation through God's gifts of Word and Sacraments. We can ask for His help, then, to be models for our children. When we attend church and Bible class regularly with joy, we affirm that these opportunities are important and a great blessing to us. When we partake frequently of the Lord's Supper, children see that we need the love and forgiveness God offers through this Sacrament. Letting children see us study Scripture daily, pray often, and seek God's guidance encourages them to do the same.

Talk

Talk with your children about God and what He has done for you: how He protects from harm, how He leads in decision making, and how He blesses each day. As you share your faith stories, your children grasp that God is bigger, more powerful, and more loving than they are. They learn to see and talk about God's actions in their lives as well.

God has appointed us to our vocation as teachers and parents, those with responsibility—and ability—to be in charge. We need to say, "You can go this far and no farther." Setting boundaries protects children from themselves, the world, and Satan's snares. Limits can include what children watch on television, when homework is done, what games they can play, and how family members talk to one another.

Results

When children experience the consequences of their actions—picking up books they pulled onto the floor, washing clean a scribbled-on wall, or finishing homework and missing a family treat—they learn that actions bring results, both good and bad.

Above all, children need to know they are forgiven and loved, even when they sin. When they are unrepentant, we point them to God's sorrow over sin. When they are repentant, we can share God's forgiveness, and ours, with them.

Children learn to be disciples by watching us, by learning what they can and cannot do, by suffering "natural" consequences of their actions, by receiving and giving forgiveness. Especially, they learn to be disciples from God's Holy Word. God bless you as you help them grow.

Think About

- My vocation as teacher includes . . .

- What can consequences for behavior teach children?

- How can you demonstrate positive discipline?

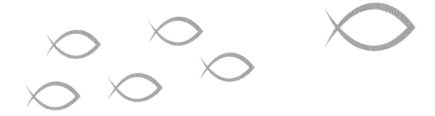

Partnering with Parents

Tom Nummela

Review

Parents are your partners as you teach God's Word to the students in your Sunday School class. The parents of your students share your desire that instruction time be productive each Sunday. They are, in all likelihood, more concerned than you are about how their children behave in Sunday School and other public places. They want their children—and the other children in your class—to have the opportunity to hear God's life-changing Word. Engage these partners in conversation before, during, and after any discipline issues you have with their children.

Contact

Take time before you begin teaching each year to contact the parents of your students for a brief telephone conversation or home visit. You certainly do not want the first contact you ever have with parents to be an explanation of why you had to remove their child from your class for discipline problems. That kind of phone call is much easier when you know the parents, have talked with them about Sunday School, and have built some connections with them.

During that initial contact, ask these partners about their children and families. What is their normal Sunday schedule? Does their child usually get breakfast on Sunday? Do they mind if snacks are served occasionally? Does their child have any food allergies? What are the child's hobbies? Does he or she like to read? Does the child have friends in your class? What Sunday School activities does he or she like most or least? Also during this visit, leave your name, phone number, and e-mail address. Invite the parents to contact you with any concerns that develop, and promise to do the same.

Keep in Touch

Don't hesitate to be in touch with parents as soon as discipline issues, even minor ones, arise. Describe the behavior you've observed and how you plan to approach the issue. Invite the parents' suggestions. Make it clear that you and they are working together in the matter of Christian education for their child.

In any serious discipline situation, you might invite one of the parents to sit in during Sunday School. Some churches invite the parents to sit in or assist in class on a regular, rotating basis. In addition to being a wonderful source of assistance for the teacher, it makes the parents' presence in class a normal thing, not an obvious punishment or ploy.

Follow up with parents after implementing any discipline plans you make together. Affirm both the student's and the parents' efforts to make the Sunday School time productive. Such regular communication will cement your partnership together and be a blessing to the children you teach.

Think About

- My students' parents probably see me as . . .

- What kinds of parent contacts are important?

- Why is it important to be proactive rather that reactive?

- Are there any parents you do not see regularly? If so, how can you reach out to them?

Shall I Tell Their Parents?

David Ebeling

OPENING THOUGHT

Did you contact the parents of the last student you reprimanded in class? Should you have?

Review

During most classes, Sunday School teachers deal with children who act out, are significantly inattentive, refuse to participate, wander away, pick on other children, or otherwise present class-management challenges. The teacher makes decisions on the spot to respond to those challenges. When the class time is over, the thought may go through your mind, "Shall I tell their parents?"

Each incident requires the teacher's judgment. The teacher considers family history, knowledge of the child's behavior patterns, severity of the problem, and impact on other children and then makes a decision.

"Shall I contact the parents?" As you consider that decision, here are some issues to consider.

Contacting the parents is probably a wise choice if

- you had earlier declared, "Do that one more time and I'll have to have a talk with your Mom."
- the child's parents had specifically asked you to inform them if there were any problems.
- it involved stealing something or hurting someone.
- you have confidence that the parents will be supportive with follow-up.
- a negative pattern of behavior is one you cannot break.

Initiating parent contact may not be necessary if

- the incident is rare and not a behavior pattern.
- your rapport with the child is such that he or she respects and accepts your discipline.
- the child is compliant with your directions and response.

- the problem is a common one for children in that stage of development.

- you have cause to believe that parent reaction would be detrimental to the child or to family dynamics.

Parents trust their children to our care for the Sunday School class time. They expect teachers to act in their stead. They trust us to teach the Word of the Lord in a way that their children can understand, and they expect us to maintain an orderly, inviting classroom. We cannot ignore bad behavior. Yet, most parents expect that we will effectively handle routine classroom management and discipline. They don't need to know every detail of what happens during class. When some incident is not routine or if a new pattern of disruption evolves, parents have a right to be informed.

"Shall I tell their parents?" You may wish to talk it over with another teacher, with your Sunday School director, or with your pastor before making a decision. Then pray for wisdom and understanding as you determine the best course of action.

Think About

- Contact the parents or not? How will you decide?

- Evaluate your last few student-discipline experiences based on this teacher/writer's guidelines.

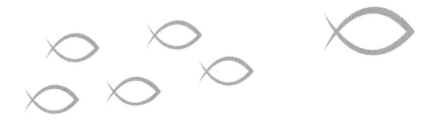

The Power of the Parent

Rebecca Fisher

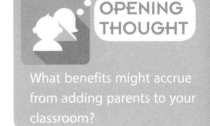

OPENING THOUGHT

What benefits might accrue from adding parents to your classroom?

Review

When we think about managing a classroom with care, we don't often immediately consider adding parents to the mix, but their presence can be a powerful tool to build stronger, more intentional bridges between faith, family, and life. We know from Scripture that parents play a role second only to the Holy Spirit in building the spiritual foundation of their children's lives. Yet, so often, Sunday School and Midweek School classes become places where children are dropped off so the church can weave its magic with the children far removed from the family unit. We have a responsibility and privilege to bring them together as often as we are able.

Connecting

Finding ways of connecting parents to the Sunday School or Midweek School classroom can be a blessing to the parents, to their children, and to the particular ministry. Too often, if parents do not feel their gift is teaching, they conclude that there is no place for them. It's our responsibility to provide a role where they can serve joyfully and successfully in their child's faith development! Consider these suggestions:

Prepare a parent panel to share life stories or faith stories related to the topic of the day. If the students are learning about Daniel in the lions' den, ask parents to tell about ways they are sometimes encouraged to turn against God in their work setting and how they handle it. Provide questions in advance to ensure more complete responses.

Sending

Send students home with parent homework. For instance, when looking at friendship formation, ask students to gather information related to their parents' best friends when they were in that grade. Students can report back, knowing more about their parents and understanding how interconnected they can be.

Ask more introverted parents to serve as small-group leaders. Develop a short list of discussion questions for each parent to ask the table of four or five students at a given time in the lesson. Assure the parents that their task is only to ask the question and probe a bit further, not to provide the "right answer" or lecture about the topic.

Using

Utilize the God-given talents of parents to organize special events, serve snacks, or make things for the classroom as carpenters or craftspeople. Truly amazing things happen when parents are invited to contribute to their children's faith journey. Parent connections help children focus on God's Word for their lives. When children witness a parent's enthusiasm and willingness to become directly involved with their spiritual development, it conveys a strong message about their value in Christ to those adults.

Now that's a well-managed classroom!

Think About

- How welcome are parents in my classroom?

- Which parents would you like to involve in your classroom?

- How could you use parents each week?

Say No to Sin

Gretchen Gebhardt

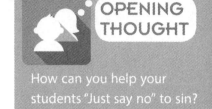
Review

"Shame on you!" After forty years, I can still hear my grandmother's words as she shook her finger at me. I still wince at her disapproval. But I never doubted that my grandmother cared for me. I knew that she loved me enough to want to help me say no to sin.

A Lost Art

The art of rebuking is often lost today. It is deemed socially unacceptable to tell someone, even a child, that they have sinned. Many teach that what is right depends on the circumstances—that sometimes it is okay to lie, cheat, steal, commit adultery, or even kill the unborn. They say, "Don't judge! Don't impose your values on others!"

This is not what God teaches. He demands that we keep every one of His commandments, without exception. God still says no to sin. But God also knows our need for a Savior. He gives us His Word and helps us grow in faith and apply His grace by saying no to sin.

Law and Gospel

As teachers we shouldn't hesitate to let God's Word do the rebuking. Look for the Law and the Gospel in every lesson you teach. When the Law is applied to our students' lives, they see their wrongdoing and recognize their sin. Then through the Gospel, the students see God's love, they are moved to confession, and they hear God's sweet words of forgiveness assuring them that Jesus died for their sins and rose from the dead in victory over sin so we can be certain of eternal life with Him.

When your children tell an offensive joke, break a rule, or boast of winning a fight, discuss it with them. Ask, "Does that joke show love?" "Why is it important to obey your parents and teachers?" "What do the commandments say about fighting?" Hold your students accountable for their actions, but be quick to speak words of forgiveness when they repent of their wrong, and encourage them with God's love through which they can say no to sin.

Think About

- Balancing Law and Gospel means . . .

- How can you properly share God's Word with students?

- How can you speak truth to students in a loving way?

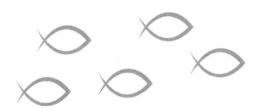

Section 5

Discipline Problems

I shall not die, but I shall live, and recount the deeds of the LORD. The LORD has disciplined me severely, but He has not given me over to death.

Open to me the gates of righteousness, that I may enter through them and give thanks to the LORD.

Psalm 118:17–19

Confession and Forgiveness in Sunday School

Paul McCain

Review

You are prepared and have a pretty good idea of what you hope to accomplish during class. You feel confident—plans made, materials organized. You know there will be routine disruptions to deal with and some time challenges. Maybe church runs a bit long, so you might have to modify your outline. Maybe the children will be more squirmy than usual. That's Sunday School teaching. You can always count on unpredictable events.

When everyone and everything is ready, you start your lesson. Things are going well when suddenly, two children get into a tug-of-war. A full-blown argument breaks out. Harsh words fly. Now what? You stop the conflict and restore order. You restore relative calm, but you notice that the two children still have red, angry faces. This disruption is an opportunity to teach and model confession and forgiveness of sins.

Sin

Our culture has a hard time with sin and, therefore, also with forgiveness. We hear about "apologies," "expressing regret," or even worse, "inappropriate behavior." Some apologies are just excuses or self-justifications. We hear "I did not intend to offend" and "if anyone was offended." We have a very carefully developed avoidance system for ducking the issues of sin and forgiveness. That is why in the Church, we must do all we can to counteract these influences.

For the children of God, saying "I'm sorry" is not a burden; it is a blessing. What is more, we are free to not only say more than simply "I'm sorry" but also "Please forgive me." What is the response to those words? Do we just shrug and say "Don't worry about it" or "It's okay"? No, we need to nurture a culture of true confession of sin and actual forgiveness of sin. We need to say, "I forgive you, and in Christ, so does God."

Forgiveness

This is never a matter simply of a pious wish or a kind thought. No, Christ has gifted each of us with the words of the Gospel, putting that word in our hearts and minds and on our lips. The Gospel, the Good News, is never merely a wish or a possibility or a kind thought. The Gospel is the actual power of God that does what it proclaims: forgiveness, life, and salvation. The Gospel always delivers what it describes; it is the power of God unto salvation.

When a conflict situation arises in the Sunday School classroom, you have the opportunity to help children learn what it is to ask for and receive forgiveness. With our children at home, when they were little, we taught them specific words to say: "I am sorry that I [fill in the blank]. Please forgive me." The response: "I forgive you, and God does too." It doesn't have to be a long, emotional exchange. Those simple words will do: "I forgive you, and God does too." As they grew older, we led them to understand more fully the meaning of those words and what a blessing they are.

It is important for us to extend forgiveness and to declare that the forgiveness we extend, God's forgiveness in Christ, is both personal and corporate. The healing words we use in our lives, "I forgive you," are predicated on the fact that we are forgiven in Christ. It is all about sinners sharing forgiveness with one another. The Church is in the business of forgiveness, not excuses. The Church's task is to absolve sin, not to justify it or overlook it. Thus, in the Sunday School classroom, after order has been restored, it would be appropriate for the teacher to have the children involved speak words of confession and forgiveness to one another. Obviously, this may not always be practical, but at least the attempt needs to be made. Younger children can grow into this practice; older children not used to it will at least be exposed to it. And then, encouragement can be given that children take this home and practice it there.

Also remind your children about what goes on in the worship service in the Confession and Absolution. If age appropriate, it would be good to use the hymnal to show children an order of Confession and Absolution that they can use with their pastor, whom God has appointed to be their spiritual shepherd. The words also serve as a model to use with one another. There are tremendous resources in the hymnal to help us articulate our shame, guilt, and need for forgiveness and then to extend to one another the powerful comfort of forgiveness in Christ.

If there is a significant and ongoing behavior problem in your classroom, deal with it. Involve the parents, the Sunday School superintendent, and, quite possibly, the pastor to make sure the disruption is not allowed to continue. It is not fair to the rest of the children when one or two children are permitted to ruin the Sunday School experience for the others. Confessing and forgiving sins is not to be used as a way to avoid dealing with an ongoing situation.

Think About

- How is saying "Please forgive me" more helpful than "I'm sorry"?

- How can Confession and Absolution from worship carry over to Sunday School?

- Why is it important for students to apologize for wrongdoing and hear the words "I forgive you"?

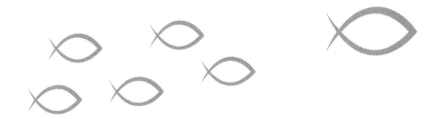

Tools For Classroom Management

Lyla Glaskey

Review

Sunday School teachers deal with the same classroom disruptions that regular classroom teachers face, but often with fewer resources. It can be frustrating when a carefully planned lesson gets derailed by the very students the teacher is trying to reach with the Gospel. A few effective tools for classroom management can make a big difference in many situations.

Winning

The first and last few minutes of class are a golden opportunity to build relationships with students. Teachers who are running late, making copies, getting organized, or going over the lesson one more time are losing precious minutes that could be spent building and strengthening student relationships. It takes mere seconds to greet, touch, and notice—and it gains valuable minutes of instruction.

- A smile, a quick touch on the top of the head or shoulder, and a personal welcome to the classroom go a long way in cultivating cooperative behavior later when the students are supposed to be listening to the lesson.

- Noticing new shoes, a personal success, or a family difficulty lets students know you care for them.

- A handshake, high five, or pat on the shoulder as students leave lets the students know their teacher still loves and cares for them, even if there were problems during class.

Even a sullen and difficult child could respond to greet, touch, and notice. For children who struggle with accepting affection or trusting adults, noticing things about them is less threatening than compliments. For these kids, a compliment may make them wonder what the teacher wants from them. If they have a negative view of themselves, they may feel the compliments are not honest. Try noticing trivial things about the child—new shoes or fresh haircut. Later you might comment on things that are a bit more personal—seeing Dad in church or noting that an aunt is in the hospital. Noticing builds relationships with these withdrawn children. Be aware, though, that touch can be misconstrued, and use it sensitively.

Losing

When teachers get into power struggles with students, especially in front of fellow students, everyone loses. Many children and young people are unwilling to back down in front of their friends, no matter how much they might actually want to. The teacher cannot win without damaging the relationship or lose without looking weak to the class. It is best to avoid power struggles whenever possible and to handle them privately when they cannot be avoided. Often, it is a matter of knowing who has control of what actions in a given situation. We can avoid power struggles and give students some positive control.

Anyone who has ever tried to get a toddler to eat something he didn't like knows that children have wills of their own. Sometimes adults invite power struggles just with the way they phrase their directions or requests. Enforceable statements are an easy way to communicate without setting the stage for trouble. Instead of telling students what to do, the teacher tells the students what he or she—the teacher—will do. The teacher avoids telling children to do something that the teacher cannot, in fact, make them do. It helps the teacher consider what aspects of the classroom experience are really within his or her control. The teacher may not be able to make the kids be quiet, but he or she can decide who gets a treat at the end of the lesson. These examples show the difference between unenforceable commands and enforceable statements:

- "Be quiet!" vs. "I will begin when it is quiet."

- "Turn to Genesis." vs. "We will be reading in Genesis."

- "Stop messing around, or you won't get any candy today!" vs. "I give candy at the end to those who listen."

- "Quit asking silly questions!" vs. "I will answer questions about other topics after class."

Choice

When offering choices, give only two options—and make sure you like both.

Some choices help prevent problems. "Would you like to use crayons or colored pencils today? Shall we sit in chairs or in a circle on the floor? Would you like to say memory individually or in pairs? Will we stand or sit to read Scripture?"

Some choices can be used to quickly stop a problem. Make sure both choices are realistic. Never give an unreasonable or sarcastic option. "Will you control that behavior now or do we need to talk about it after class? Would you like to share that toy or shall I put it away for the day? Would you like to walk to opening or tiptoe?"

Caution! When using choices to deal with a problem, it is easy to fall into a power struggle. To avoid a power struggle, these hints can make all the difference.

- Keep your voice and attitude calm and pleasant. If you show anger or frustration, you are making the problem yours instead of the student's.

- Assume the child is going to choose the least severe option. Do not wait for an answer. Give the choice, assume he or she will straighten up, and keep teaching.

- Remember the advice about enforceable statements. Demanding eye contact will create a power struggle.

Once when a teacher was speaking to a parent after class, the mother's three-year-old got very interested in the toys in the classroom. When the parent tried to leave, the little girl didn't want to go. A power struggle such as only a strong-willed toddler can create ensued. The teacher knelt down next to the child and gave a simple choice: "Would you like to walk to the sanctuary holding Mommy's hand or would you like to hold mine?" The little tyke got the control she was craving, and Mommy got to church on time. The mother thought the teacher had worked some kind of magic spell. It wasn't magic. It was offering choices.

Think About

- How does giving a child a choice also help the child's behavior to be in control?

- How are tone and content of your message important?

- Record phrases you hear yourself saying; how could you change them to be more positive?

Managing Misbehavior

Marlene Krohse

OPENING THOUGHT

Yelling in class is bad . . . by both students and teachers.

Review

Jimmy is yelling because Ryan won't share the glue. Ashanti's feelings are hurt because you didn't pick the song she wanted to sing, and now she won't sing at all. Jenny and Olivia are yelling at each other and won't stop. José and Sam are having a poking contest. No one appears to be listening. All you can think of teaching this morning is how sin affects our daily lives. Fortunately, not all of these situations occur at the same time. What can you do when you experience these behaviors in Sunday School?

Learning Control

Young children are working on learning to control their behavior. This takes time, practice, and encouragement. Begin by letting the children know what behavior is expected. Is it time for them to sit quietly? Try beginning with a little song or finger play to shake out the wiggles and focus their attention. Let them know this is the time to listen to the story and explain what you mean. Be realistic, though—little bodies have difficulty sitting absolutely still. If you have a particular child that struggles to pay attention or keep on task, move that child close to you when you tell the story, or give them something to do to keep them focused. If your class is noisy, try lowering your voice. Sometimes when we get louder, so do they! Engage them with action or inflection in your voice. If your class is particularly squirmy or inattentive, try varying where or how you tell the story. If it's time to sing, remind the children to use a pleasant voice and model the behavior.

Learning Consequences

Young children may have difficulty seeing the consequences of their actions. This often leads to problems between individual children. Help them give words to their feelings. Encourage them to tell each other what is bothering them, such as, "I don't like it when you take the stickers from me." After the comment is made and the other child responds, the situation is over. This can be a great opportunity to practice repentance and forgiveness.

Often, there is no need to call attention to misbehavior or administer correction. Simply distract and redirect the students to other activities. If an activity is getting completely out of hand, end it. You may be able to restart it another time. Note what type of activities work well with your class, such as singing a quiet song or doing some physical activity; use it when necessary to settle down the group.

Encourage them to treat each other with kindness, and help them grow in their interactions with others as children of the King.

Think About

- I model good behavior in my classroom by . . .

- What are some practical ways to redirect students' negative behavior?

- Why is it important to teach children how to respond to each other with appropriate behavior?

Handling Misbehavior

Rodney Rathmann

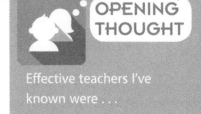
Review

Teaching Sunday School, bringing God's truth to children, is a high calling. Many children have no other opportunity to read, discuss, and learn God's Word.

However, teachers with an idealized notion of children—enthusiastically responding to them, full of acceptance and appreciation, and eager to share Jesus' love with others—are likely to meet with occasional disappointment. Many such teachers end up leaving the Sunday School classroom bitter and disillusioned. Effective teachers are those with a realistic understanding of children and their behaviors when with their peers.

Like all of us, our students are sinners. They need to hear the convicting words of the Law when they misbehave as well the sweet assurance of the Gospel for the sinful actions of which they repent. They need someone mature in faith, love, and understanding to provide them with a safe, consistent, Gospel-centered learning environment where they can grow together in faith and knowledge as the Holy Spirit nurtures them through God's Word. Sharing the love of Jesus as a Christian teacher involves dealing appropriately with classroom management issues as they occur.

Fire Extinguisher or Fire Safety?

Some teachers handle disruptive behaviors with the fire extinguisher approach, waiting until misbehavior occurs before considering how misbehaviors ought to be handled. Effective discipline suggests a fire safety approach, planning and teaching ahead of time about discipline and growing students as disciples.

Children know that standards for appropriate behavior vary. The behavior that is appropriate for children singing around a campfire differs from behavior that is appropriate for children singing a choral anthem during church. Successful teachers take time at the beginning of the year to establish clear behavioral expectations for their classrooms.

They keep the rules few, simple, and easy to remember, sometimes posting them in the room. Examples:

- We will respect one another.

- We will cooperate in activities designed to help us learn God's Word.

- We will show our love for God, His Word, and His house.

At some grade levels, students can help to establish classroom rules. Once established, classroom standards need to be consistently maintained. A system of rewards and consequences can be set up and applied. Again, older students can help establish these. Rewards may consist of celebrations such as receiving a special snack the Sunday after cooperative behavior. Consequences may consist of having to move to a time-out corner or the loss of a special privilege.

Student Needs

All students want to feel successful as participants in the classroom. They want others, including the teacher, to recognize, acknowledge, and appreciate their successes. Common causes of misbehavior relate to students' inability to achieve success in receiving attention, exercising power, and realizing self-confidence.

Students craving attention are often the ones who speak without permission, make outlandish comments, or engage in noisy behavior. These students can divert the attention of the rest of the class away from the Bible story and planned lesson.

Students acting out in a quest for power may be openly defiant, refusing to follow rules and adding controversy. Such students will try to lead the group in inappropriate ways. Students seeking power may directly compete with a teacher.

Some students feel inadequate. They may be new to the Christian faith and therefore unfamiliar with Bible knowledge and faith concepts. They may have reading difficulties or other learning problems. Such students may seem uncooperative or disinterested.

Students with unmet needs in one or more of the above areas may act inappropriately toward the teacher, other students, the lesson materials, or the property of the church.

Sunday School students are most likely to find their needs met by a teacher who shows genuine interest in them. By making the effort to get to know students, teachers may be able to identify the specific needs of individual children and find creative ways to meet needs that might otherwise lead to disruptive class behavior. For example, children who crave attention might be recruited to lead some of the lesson activities. Teachers show they care in the following ways.

- They talk with students before, after, and during class about their interests, helping students to connect every event in their lives with their identities as children of God.

- They are informed about the special events in the life of each child, such as school, family, sports, music and drama events, and other activities important to the student. They reassure their students with the knowledge that Jesus is with them throughout the activities and events of their lives, forgiving, sustaining, and renewing them through the power of His Word.

- They encourage students and their parents with descriptions of positive contributions and expressions of faith observed in Sunday School.

- They deal with inappropriate behavior.

Effective Management

Effective classroom management research suggests that students appreciate teachers who demonstrate that they are in charge of the class and of the learning environment. Such teachers deal directly with disciplinary problems but in fair, consistent, and appropriate ways. Strategies successfully employed in dealing with inappropriate behaviors include the following.

- Make eye contact. Let the student know you are aware of the inappropriate action.

- Tell the student directly what appropriate behavior you want him or her to do. The focus is on the appropriate behavior desired, not the inappropriate behavior observed.

- Use a physical gesture, such as subtly shaking your head to bring the student's behavior back into line.

- Move closer to the student. This action indicates to the student your desire for his or her behavior to change immediately.

- Move the student to a time-out area to think through what has happened. Talk with him or her about the behavior. If the child says he or she is sorry, remind the child of the full and complete forgiveness Jesus won for us on Calvary and assure him or her of your forgiveness.

- Talk with, text, or phone the parents of the misbehaving child. Assure them of your love and concern for the child, describe their child's misbehavior, and enlist their help. As the primary teachers of their child, parents have a right to know of your difficulties with their child. Most will want to help.

- Enlist the help of your Sunday School superintendent or other teachers. Brainstorm together possible solutions, such as a smaller class size.

As you deal with all aspects of making disciples of the children entrusted to your care, pray. Pray regularly and often; pray for each child by name. And trust. Trust that God, who sent His only Son to earn forgiveness for all sins, forgives also the mistakes that you have made in your teaching. Trust that He who sees and knows everything will work good from all the interactions in your class—even those you do not consider your best moments in teaching. Trust in His power to bring the Good News to others through you.

Think About

- Setting standards is best followed by . . .

- How are the "fire extinguisher" and "fire safety" approaches different?

- Which of the author's suggestions seem most practical for you to implement?

Facing Discipline

Lyla Glaskey

Review

When a problem arises, not only do we want to hand the problem back to the child, but we also want to keep from escalating the problem. There are several misconceptions that can worsen the problem rather than minimize them.

One of the most common and dangerous misconceptions involves eye contact. For an adult, getting a student's eye contact means gaining their attention and respect. For many students, eye contact can escalate a relatively minor problem into a confrontation. Power struggles should be avoided whenever possible because they are a lose-lose situation. Either the child loses face in front of his peers, or you do. In either case, the relationship suffers, and so does the class.

Forced Response

Forcing the child to answer or respond to you regarding misbehavior may also escalate the situation. As an adult, you may simply be checking to make sure the child understands what you expect. This works with an extremely compliant child, but those are usually not the kids acting up in Sunday School. With a misbehaving child, you may get the verbal response you want, but the child may be thinking about ways to get back at you. As one little boy explained after his teacher thought she won a power struggle with him, "I may be sitting on the outside, but I'm standing on the inside!"

By stopping just past the child, you avoid confrontational eye contact. By whispering, even if the other kids hear you, you create a sense of confidentiality. Most kids will not need to save face about something whispered to them, even if the other students heard it. By moving away without waiting for a response, you assume the student will comply. Most of the time, the student will. The assumption of compliance is a powerful and effective tool. Not only will most students respond, but it also preserves the student-teacher relationship.

Circulate

One last suggestion: Avoid teaching only from the front of the room. Circulate around the room while you teach. You can move in to handle a problem more easily and inconspicuously. This will also help prevent misbehavior! In some situations, you might get a disrespectful response, and now have an even tougher all-out power struggle situation to face. All-out struggles are tough to manage, so do all you can to remain calm and prevent this type of scenario. Instead of confrontation, try this:

- When you need to speak to a child about misbehavior in front of his or her peers, it is best to avoid eye contact and not wait for a response.

- Try approaching the child slowly, with a pleasant expression—and ideally, while still teaching.

- Stop just past the child, lean down, and whisper what you need to say.

- Keep moving and continue teaching.

Think About

- In discipline situations, eye contact can . . .

- What kinds of visual and auditory prompts are important for discipline?

- How does your location in the classroom affect student behavior?

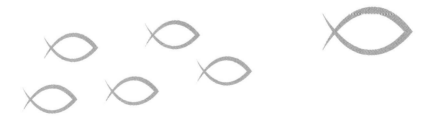

Like a River

Rebecca Fisher

Review

OPENING THOUGHT

An alternative to stopping a child's negative behavior might be to . . .

While vacationing in Colorado this summer, I had the opportunity to spend many hours watching the Snake River while my young children joyfully hurled hundreds of rocks into the flow. I had many thoughts while watching that river, but this one stands out: if you wish to alter the flow of a river, don't try to stop it, but rather find a way to channel it in another direction.

Like a river, our students have energy that seems unending. Both babble nonstop. It's both foolish and frustrating to attempt to stop a river from flowing. The same thing is true of the energy pouring from our children. Often in our classrooms, that energy seems to flood the room, and enthusiastic chaos ensues. The wise teacher will help students redirect this enthusiasm rather than stifle it. Here are four quick suggestions for channeling energy more productively.

- **Change gears.** This is an effective strategy with older children as well as toddlers. If attention wanes during discussion, or if an activity begins to get out of control, transition to the next activity or revise your approach. Do this without anger, irritation, or sarcasm. The goal is to change gears naturally. For example, if the attention is far from the movie clip you are showing, stop the clip early, and ask what the students think will happen next. Surprise is a powerful tool for redirecting children.

- **Move the students around.** If they're not focused on what you're doing, shift their focus by shifting what you're having them do. If you've had them sitting in a large group, have them break up into smaller randomly selected groups for the next section. If they've been unresponsive to questions, have them move to the "agree" or "disagree" side of the room as you make statements about the lesson.

- **Divert attention inward.** Give them a situation to consider or a part in a role play. This not only captures their attention but also is a powerful tool for integrating faith into their personal lives.

- **Change your approach.** Instead of talking loudly to get their attention, try getting quieter. Instead of standing in one familiar place, move about the classroom. Instead of calling on volunteers, try pulling names out of a hat. Rivers will flow. That's part of their charm. The energy in children will pour forth. We wouldn't want it any other way. But our role as teachers is often to divert that energy productively toward growth in faith and Christian understanding.

May He enable you to redirect the river flowing from those you teach.

Think About

- Redirecting a student might be most helpful in my classroom when . . .

- Which of the four suggestions will you implement first and why?

- Why is the skill of redirecting important?

Forgiveness

Matthew C. Harrison

Review

I don't know your parenting sins, but I know pretty much all of my own (and what I don't recall, my dear wife and two boys could call to my attention with some detail!). For instance, not long ago there was an incident involving my eleven-year-old son's errant golf ball, the bunion on my right toe, and my attempts to assuage my pain by throttling my own son. Thankfully, I didn't hurt him. We both quickly found some humor in the situation, and the laughter did wonders for my pain. But I had acted inappropriately out of anger. I had sinned.

Never Assumed

Martin Luther wrote (Large Catechism, Fourth Commandment) that the teacher stands in the place of the parent, in the place of God. Sinning against parent or teacher is sinning against God. A parent or teacher abusing authority, exasperating a child, is likewise a breaking of the Fourth Commandment. Standing in the place of God would be an unbearable and even horrible task without forgiveness. But there is glorious freedom in being a Christian parent. We are free not to expect ourselves or our children to be perfect. We are free to confess our sins to our children when we fall short and free to hear our children confess wrongdoing—to be absolved, and to absolve them—in the name of Jesus. That is the most fundamental Christian truth taught in our homes and Christian schools.

Forgiveness Spoken

In our household, midst the myriad tasks and lessons of parenthood, forgiveness is spoken, not assumed. None of this "let's just forget it" business! There are appropriate consequences for sinful actions, but forgiveness is always spoken. It must be spoken. Jesus gave forgiveness to us to be spoken.

At church, He gave us pastors so nothing would be in doubt about the forgiveness He speaks to us (*Luther's Small Catechism with Explanation*, Confession, p. 29). We are forgiven no matter how we feel inside! Parents and children speak that same forgiveness in our homes and families to each other (Matthew 18:15–18). How much pain and sorrow and anguish could be avoided in our families and churches if only we would speak forgiveness to each other! The context for teaching as parents has to be one of spoken forgiveness. This means we know sin is a struggle in the Christian life (Romans 7:14–25), both in the lives of our children and in ourselves. And it means we live to forgive, no matter what our vocation in life. And in the midst of our weaknesses come joy and love.

My eleven-year-old has long since spoken forgiveness for my "bunion incident." And we love each other all the more. That's a lesson worth teaching, and the Lord did it through a sinful parent this time.

Think About

- What would "forgiveness spoken" look like in my classroom?

- In what ways are parenting and teaching alike?

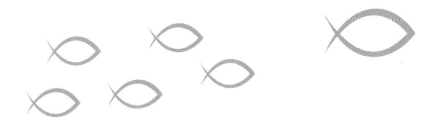

Section6

Discipline for Different Ages

Children, obey your parents in the Lord, for this is right. "Honor your father and mother" (this is the first commandment with a promise), "that it may go well with you and that you may live long in the land." Fathers, do not provoke your children to anger, but bring them up in the discipline and instruction of the Lord.

Ephesians 6:1–4

The Art of Discipline

Drew Gerdes

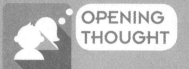

OPENING THOUGHT

What is the connection between discipline for little ones and their level of development?

Review

Ah—the joys of teaching young children! Many have a difficult time sitting still, some talk louder inside than they do in the backyard, and some have no idea that crayons are not for chewing. Some days, you may rethink your position as Sunday School teacher. You wonder if saying the same thing ten times is really worth it. Is chasing after little Tommy as he runs from the classroom really a fun way to spend a Sunday morning? While teaching young children certainly can be challenging, it is also a very rewarding experience full of faith-filled blessings!

Young children are members of our congregation too and deserve the same educational opportunities as older members. The children in your class come from many different backgrounds and homes. Not all children listen well, follow directions, and remember all the details you would prefer they do. As frustrating as it may seem, children need to move to think. Teachers of young children must remember the different ability levels of various ages. Understanding the diverse children we work with leads to easier classroom management and more enjoyable lessons.

Appropriate Tasks

Do a little homework, and find a list of appropriate tasks the children you work with should be able to accomplish. A simple Google search of "age-appropriate tasks" or "developmental behaviors" should give you a worthwhile list and start you in the right direction.

Do some people in your congregation or family consider you a bit odd for teaching young children? Consider it an honor! God has chosen you to help guide these children as they grow in their faith. You are important in the process of their faith development. It's obvious you enjoy being around little children, playing with them, and helping them learn about Jesus! God never said life would be easy, but when you are serving Him, He will give you the guidance you need.

When you begin to feel down or inadequate for the task, remember that you are doing God's work. Not everyone is gifted to teach young children. God chose you! Accept the task He gives you gladly!

Be Clear

As you reflect on your classroom interactions, remember to be consistent. Set clear, developmentally and age-appropriate expectations. Remember, you only have these kids for a short period of time. Make the most of it! These children are in your class to learn about Jesus; this should be the highest priority.

Discipline does not mean getting crabby, yelling, or becoming frustrated. In our environment of working with young children, discipline means helping children learn not just about Jesus, but also about right and wrong; the proper way to accomplish tasks; how to interact with others; and so on. We help children learn to control emotions, impulses, and many other areas of their development.

No child is ever perfect, but neither are we! Sin entered this world and, unfortunately, is here to stay. How thankful we are that Jesus died and rose again to pay the price for our sins. We *all*—not just little children—need discipline. Say a prayer today and ask the Holy Spirit to guide your teaching and classroom discipline, all so little children can know more about Jesus and the Gospel message!

Think About

- How is discipline with young students unique?

- What is the most important thing to remember from this essay?

- What brings you joy as you teach God's children?

Discipline for Preschoolers

Judy Williams

OPENING THOUGHT

In what way does your teaching start well before class begins?

Review

Teaching young children about God's love can be fun. Most children come eager to learn. But what do you do when a child resists joining in the worship and Bible story? What's the best way to handle a child who constantly interrupts?

The easiest way to have an orderly classroom is to plan ahead. Make a weekly schedule and use it consistently; children benefit from a familiar routine. Recruit a parent or teenage volunteer as a helper.

As you begin preparing for the following Sunday, pray that God would help you teach and that the Holy Spirit will open the hearts of the children to His Word. As you plan, give preference to the activities the children will find most interesting. Provide lots of pre-session materials because young children do not share well; this will reduce conflict.

Being Proactive

On Sunday morning, arrive early so you are ready when the children arrive. Greet each arriving child and get him or her interested in a project or activity.

Once in a while, you will have a child who hits or shouts. Calmly but firmly, tell the child this behavior is not acceptable and suggest an alternative way to express his or her feelings.

When you are ready to begin the lesson, let the children know they need to finish their presession activity. When time is up, chant or sing a cleanup rhyme. If a child is reluctant to help, suggest something specific he or she can do, such as putting away the red crayons while you put away the blue ones. Compliment the children on their efforts.

For worship and Bible story, invite the children to come and sit where everyone can see you. Some teachers like to have the children sit on individual carpet samples to define space and keep children from bothering each other.

Remind the children that it's time to listen and do what you say. If a child interrupts, put your index finger to your closed lips and shake your head no. If this doesn't work, suggest that your helper sit next to the child.

If you serve a snack, have it ready so the children do not have to wait; waiting is hard at this age. Thank God for the food. After the children finish the snack, let them throw napkins and cups in a garbage can before joining you once again in the worship area.

Continue with familiar songs or action poems until all the children have joined you. Then begin the closing ritual—reviewing the Bible verse, prayer, and singing. Check to make sure all children have their belongings before leaving the room.

When you have your lesson well planned and maintain a balance of firmness and friendliness, you reduce the number of discipline problems in the classroom. You'll have fun sharing the story of Jesus' love, and your students will enjoy learning.

Think About

- Good presession planning means . . .

- Why is routine so important for young children?

- What role does good planning play in dealing with young children?

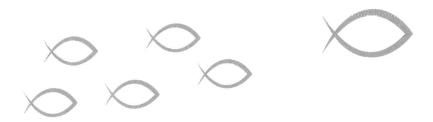

Disciplined Teens

Julie Stiegemeyer

Review

Do the words *disciplined teen* seem like an oxymoron? Aren't teens by nature rebellious and undisciplined? We all remember the angst of those confusing years.

Discipline problems at any age can affect the whole class. The teacher can't communicate the Bible lesson. The disruptive ones frustrate other students. Students may even tune out since they're not getting anything out of the lesson. Tackle discipline with a four-step approach.

Prayer: Whatever your concern, start with prayer. Pray that God will open your students' hearts to be receptive to His Word and that He will guide you in sharing the Gospel message.

Preparation: Prepare thoroughly so you can move smoothly from activity to activity without lag time. Students stay attentive. Organize your classroom; a room that is a jumble of books, choir robes, and old Christmas costumes might foster disorderly conduct among the students. Discipline sometimes improves when students sit in chairs around a table rather than on the youth room couches. (Save the couches for free time at the end of your Sunday School hour.)

Standards: Have rules for classroom behavior clear in your own mind. Here are some suggestions.

- **Be respectful**—Treat the teacher and your fellow students with Christian care.

- **Be attentive**—Disruptive or overly loud behavior is not appropriate.

- **Be safe**—Do not endanger the well-being of yourself or any others.

These are common-sense standards that can be more narrowly defined for your classroom.

Communication: Once you have guidelines for appropriate behavior outlined in your own mind, communicate your expectations. At the beginning of the year, make clear what you think is appropriate behavior. Post your guidelines and remind your students of them as necessary. Stick with your guidelines throughout the school year. Also, communicate the consequences of misbehavior. If students know what is expected and those expectations are consistently reinforced, they are more likely to abide by your rules.

It's easy for disciplinarians to lapse into legalisms when dealing with behavior issues in the classroom, but remember to focus on the Gospel as you deal with unruly kids. Christ died When the righteous increase, the people rejoice, for their sins too, and it's a teacher's joy to share that Good News— even with disagreeable teens!

Think About

- Teens need . . .

- What standards would you set for the teens in your class?

- How could you prevent lapsing into legalistic leadership?

- How can you more narrowly define the standards listed?

One Size Does NOT Fit All!

Rebecca Fisher

Review

I always chuckle when I read "One size fits all" on a clothing item. Clever marketing, perhaps, but there will always be someone that the product will not fit.

The same is true in our classrooms. For instance, biblical knowledge spans quite a continuum. In your classroom, there may be one student who doesn't yet know Noah and others who can name, in rapid succession, his wife, his children, the mountaintop where they landed, and why some animals came in groups of seven. Could one size of question or instruction fit all these background abilities? It is doubtful.

Difficulties

Management difficulties occur when students aren't focused on and engaged with the material you are sharing with them. This can happen both when students are bored with repetition of things they already know and when they are frustrated because it seems like everyone else knows what's going on in this lesson except them. When this happens, they find something else to do and often distract others as well.

Clothing needs to be tailored to fit snugly, and so does your instruction, if you want students to stay focused and minimize any disruptions. Humans learn best with moderate challenges. Students who consistently fail lose their motivation to learn. Students who succeed too easily also lose their motivation to learn.

Customizing

Try ranking your students in three groups based on knowledge of the biblical accounts. Then consider distributing different types of questions or offering different projects that might challenge each group.

For instance, when we teach David and Goliath to fifth graders, we might give this assignment to students with little background knowledge: "After skimming over the Bible account, tell who you think the main and supporting characters were, and act out the main event for the class." Students with some background might be asked to describe the feelings of the Israelite army when they were listening to Goliath's taunts and write a journal entry from that perspective.

Finally, those who know this story inside and out might be asked, "How was Goliath like bullies in your school? How is David's situation unique?" With some care given to the starting knowledge levels of students in your classroom, you can construct great questions and provide just the right amount of challenge to your students.

Why is this a management and discipline strategy? Fully engaged students don't have time or the inclination to disrupt a class. One size does not fit all, but we can create many sizes, one of which will fit each person.

Think About

- Asking "Does it fit?" requires knowledge about your students. What are some ways to gain additional information about them?

- If you ranked your students into three groups by biblical knowledge, who would be in each group?

- How does dividing students into groups help manage behavior?

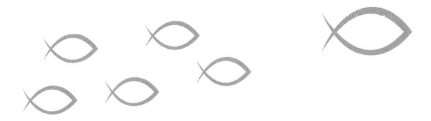

Godly Discipline

James Gimbel

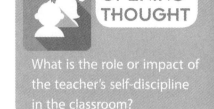

OPENING THOUGHT

What is the role or impact of the teacher's self-discipline in the classroom?

Review

Good classroom discipline is one of the most important factors in successfully including everyone. Usually, when people mention discipline, they are looking for remedial strategies—a plan to rein in a runaway classroom of students or a quick set of corrective rewards or punishments that justly and fairly modify bad behaviors. However, the first steps in discipline are not remedial, but preventive.

Preventive Discipline

Two aspects of preventive discipline that have great impact are a teacher's self-discipline and a teacher's classroom management. First, a teacher's self-discipline begins with a clear commitment not only to God in Christ but also to investing the time to read and thoroughly know the Bible account and be familiar with the Teacher Guide study notes. It also takes self-discipline to gather and prepare the classroom materials well enough in advance so they can be quickly distributed for classroom use. It includes having talking points ready for an accurate telling and authentic question-and-answer time as well as having the other activities prepared and ready to implement.

This leads to the second part of preventive classroom discipline—good class time management. Students struggle when expected to sit quietly while teachers scramble to get ready for the next activity. Inactivity can quickly breed distracted mischief, which can lead to chaos. All students, regardless of ability and personal function, respond best when things flow in an orderly routine that unfolds creatively. This involves a clearly detailed lesson plan that includes standard elements and fresh and creative approaches to exploring the lesson points in ways that connect with all learning styles. It takes balancing standard components with enough variety to keep students from being bored. It means all materials and resources are within reach, and transitions from one element to the next are thoughtful.

Student Perspective

I once asked a Sunday School student what she had learned in class. Her response? "Sit down and shut up." The teacher was better than that, but sadly, this illustrates how addressing disruptive behavior can sometimes "steal" the learning.

For those times when students get out of control, rely on God's design—showing justice (being fair and equitably attempting to have the punishment fit the crime) and showing mercy (at times, being lenient in the same spirit that God withholds punishment from us). Law and Gospel are advanced but effective tools for classroom discipline. Spontaneous displays of grace (undeserved gifts) can show students that you love and care for them and want to treat them as God does.

Godly discipline is a challenge, but it starts with managing self and the classroom. All glory goes to God where preparation and discipline are an inclusive means to growth in God's kingdom.

Think About

- What might my students remember about the last couple of classes I've taught?

- How does your self-discipline affect your classroom discipline?

- How are leniency and grace different?